Love
Has
Seven
Colors

"This book is a gift for the heart. Taking us on a journey into love, it maps out our light bodies and gives us simple but profound practices that support us in becoming truly human—spirit and body. It is a clear and thorough guide for beginners and those already versed in the perennial wisdom."

FAY BARRATT, FOUNDER AND VISIONARY
FOR THE MARY MAGDALENE SCHOOL OF WISDOM

"Jack Angelo has again created a beautifully written book. *Love Has Seven Colors* is easy to read and yet profound in its contents. The exercises provide practical ways of putting theory into practice in a powerful way. I thoroughly recommend Jack's latest book— whether you are new to spiritual concepts or an experienced practitioner, this book is a must!"

ROGER FORD, COFOUNDER AND
EXECUTIVE DIRECTOR OF THE
HEALING IN AMERICA SCHOOL OF ENERGY HEALING

"This is a very beautiful, inspiring, and wise book. Written by one of Europe's most experienced healers, Jack Angelo takes readers into the very heart and soul of energy healing and spiritual anatomy. Always compassionate and sensitive, the exercises and advice are practical and can be used immediately. Highly recommended."

WILLIAM BLOOM, PH.D.,
DIRECTOR OF THE SPIRITUAL COMPANIONS TRUST AND
AUTHOR OF *THE POWER OF THE NEW SPIRITUALITY*

Love
Has
Seven
Colors

Heart-Centered Practices
for the Energy Centers

Jack Angelo

Bear & Company
Rochester, Vermont • Toronto, Canada

Bear & Company
One Park Street
Rochester, Vermont 05767
www.BearandCompanyBooks.com

Text stock is SFI certified

Bear & Company is a division of Inner Traditions International

Library of Congress Cataloging-in-Publication Data
Names: Angelo, Jack, author.
Title: Love has seven colors : heart-centered practices for the energy centers / Jack Angelo.
Description: Rochester, Vermont : Bear & Company, 2017. | Includes bibliographical references and index.
Identifiers: LCCN 2016046316 (print) | LCCN 2017002852 (e-book) | ISBN 9781591432753 (pbk.) | ISBN 9781591432760 (e-book)
Subjects: LCSH: Spiritual life. | Love—Miscellanea. | Chakras. | Colors—Miscellanea. | Energy medicine.
Classification: LCC BL624 .A537 2017 (print) | LCC BL624 (e-book) | DDC131—dc23
LC record available at https://lccn.loc.gov/2016046316

Printed and bound in the United States by Lake Book Manufacturing, Inc. The text stock is SFI certified. The Sustainable Forestry Initiative® program promotes sustainable forest management.

10   9   8   7   6   5   4   3   2   1

Text design and layout by Virginia Scott Bowman
This book was typeset in Garamond Premier Pro with Trajan Pro, Avenir, and Helvetica used as display typefaces

To send correspondence to the author of this book, mail a first-class letter to the author c/o Inner Traditions • Bear & Company, One Park Street, Rochester, VT 05767, and we will forward the communication, or contact the author directly at **www.jackangelo.net**.

CONTENTS

PART 2

The Seven Energy Centers: Our Human Rainbow

�֍

LIST OF EXERCISES

The Pilgrimage Actions

Note: The activities in this book are called Pilgrimage Actions because they are designed to assist you on the quest, or pilgrimage, for heart-centeredness. They may be practiced alone, but if you have any kind of respiratory problems or breathing allergies or are undergoing any form of medical treatment, you should consult your medical practitioner before you proceed. The activities should not be used for purposes other than those specified.

No more than three activities should be practiced at any one session. Read through each Pilgrimage Action before starting. When practicing any of the activities for the first time, you may find it helpful to work with a pilgrim friend who can monitor your progress and, where appropriate, talk you through an activity. If no one is available, make a recording of yourself reading them.

ACKNOWLEDGMENTS

MY THANKS to Jon Graham for his continued encouragement, and to Jamaica Burns Griffin and all the team at Inner Traditions • Bear & Company for their dedicated approach. Special thanks to Jan Angelo for her inspired title, creative guidance, and patient review of the manuscript.

Note to the Reader

To make the text nongender-specific, this book uses the terms *they*, *their*, and *them*, instead of *he/she*, *his/hers*, *him/her*, unless it is obvious that a person of a certain gender is being referred to. I have capitalized certain words in the text to indicate that they are aspects of the same spiritual reality. For example: *Oneness*, *Source*, *God*, and also *Light*, *Nature*, *Earth*, *Earth Family*. When *oneness* is not capitalized it means the state of being at one or together with others.

PROLOGUE

Soul is not bothered
what race you are, what tribe you are, what family you are
or if you have no family at all.
Soul is not bothered
if you have a religion or don't have a religion.
Soul is not bothered
what kind of skin you have, what gender you have,
or what mixture of genders you have.
Soul is not bothered
if you are good or bad, courageous or cowardly,
a hero or an ordinary person.
Soul is not bothered
what age you are, whether you are abled or disabled,
clever or not, intelligent or not, smart or otherwise.
Soul is not bothered
about what you achieve or what you do not achieve.
Soul has no regrets.
Soul is not bothered
if you can't imagine,
if you never find love,
or if you never offer love or compassion.
Soul is not bothered.

But you are bothered
because you chose to be a human being
and somehow you know that Soul is within.
You are bothered because Soul is infinite breathing life
and infinite breathing life is you.
Soul is you and you are Soul.
Everyone is chosen, all of life is chosen,
was chosen, will be chosen,
but Soul is not bothered.
Soul is all-encompassing, unconditional love.

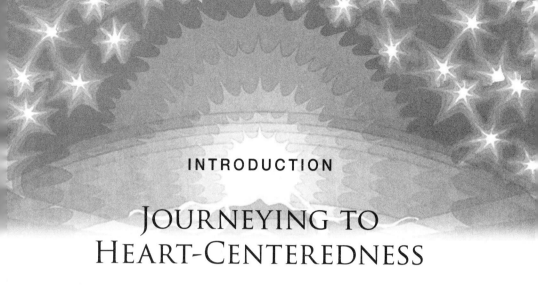

JOURNEYING TO HEART-CENTEREDNESS

LOVE HAS SEVEN COLORS presents the core wisdom practice of the ancient mystery schools—the Inner Circle Teachings on heart-centeredness—in an approach tailored to our times. The ancient teachings stress that the human mind alone cannot find the way forward out of our human dilemmas. This means retraining the mind so that it can facilitate the love-based rather than the fear-based response. The solution is to become heart centered and guided by the wisdom of the soul.

Love Has Seven Colors explains how unconditional love positively affects one's subtle energy system, especially the energy centers (chakras). In each center, these effects dispel our various illusions about life and present positive challenges for change. This book offers a powerful path to physical, psychological, and spiritual healing and wholeness. With an emphasis on personal experience, the exercises (Pilgrimage Actions) guide you through the process of achieving heart-centeredness and recovering soul presence.

JOURNEYING TOGETHER

Soul assures us that the meaning of life is in the living, that life itself is a sacred journey, for some a pilgrimage. Pilgrimage has been known down the centuries as a journey from one place to another, from one physical place on the Earth to another. Such journeys have always symbolized our inner need to journey from one state of consciousness to another—from that of the personality-mind to the sacred within. And on this quest, since life within our universe is a process, you will need to welcome the unpredictable, the unplanned, the temporary, the strange, the unfamiliar, the ambiguous, and the provisional.

The practice of heart-centeredness recovers your own sacred, unclouded vision. You will develop a connection between your brain and your heart center as those areas of the human brain that are still underused, despite thousands of years of evolution, become activated. Soul teaches that the brain has areas of underuse because human activities have not been guided by the heart but by the dominance of conditioned minds. Your practice will reveal a vision of soul, your heart, and each energy center, building a new vision of yourself and the world.

KEEP AN EXPERIENCE JOURNAL

In all my books I suggest keeping a journal because it becomes more than a record of your experiences, also providing a useful focus, even a theme, for your progress. Your journal is a record. It can include reflections and comments, accounts of meet-ups with others, and things that resonate for you. When you may not want to use words, your own drawings, images, objects you come across, and of course, anything that evokes serendipity are called for.

ABOUT WORDS—
THE LANGUAGE OF THE BOOK

The French philosopher Maurice Merleau-Ponty (1908–1961) made a study of language. He concluded that a language is not only informed by the human body, its perceptions, and its particular human community but also by every aspect of the environment with which these interact. Each language, birthed through a people's felt experience of the world, is a kind of song, a particular way of singing the world. The sounds, signs, and symbols adopted by the people become the vessels that embody their song of the world.

Often we have to use words for things and feelings that are beyond words and we sense that the words are inadequate for what we would like to convey. The word *soul* is a good example. Chapter 1 defines the word in relation to how it will be used in this book.

From the heart's viewpoint, words are vocalized sacred breath, expressing the eternally dynamic and interpenetrating aspects of the cosmos. From this viewpoint, *heaven,* for example, is not a place but a level of spiritual realization, a state of being, where the vibrating essence of the cosmos is experienced as the complementary principle of Earth, a physical level of being. Both are aspects of the same Oneness, not different places.

Words can have many meanings or nuances according to who is using them and according to who is hearing or reading them, so it is important for you, the reader, to try to sense the *energy* of the text, its "song," and not simply analyze the language alone.

In the classic of Taoism, the *Tao de Jing,* Lao Tsu (fifth and sixth centuries BCE) warns that language is a poor vehicle to carry a shift in consciousness, especially the shift in consciousness that connects mind with the heart and soul. For this reason, knowing that writing may lead to dogma, many great teachers have left it to others to do the writing. So we find their recorded sayings filled with forms that are flexible enough to adapt to the changing needs of any society, in any time. The call was always to return to the wisdom of the heart, where soul reality reveals the hidden gems of meaning in the metaphors, similes, parables, allusions, and stories used by spiritual teachers. However, a message of love conveyed in sacred writings is protected by love. This enables it to be found when hidden because of adverse circumstances, or to encourage readers to abandon mind and seek the text's message via heart perception.

HOW TO MAKE THE BEST
OF YOUR "PILGRIMAGE"

The first practice is to live your life, to learn how to live here with the Earth and the Earth Family. When you set off on the journey of practice, a new adventure begins and a new perspective arrives as old attachments disappear to make way for new experiences. Your outlook on life now includes spiritual realities and the changes within you are mirrored in the changes you see in the outer world. Practice is simply about getting in touch with your soul self—not your mind, or your feelings, or your body, but with a sense of the presence that animates them. It is essential to follow the promptings of your heart, not the urgent suggestions of your mind or the mind of another. Then each action and each intention can be an expression of the sacred. Practice is an experience, not an intellectual exercise or hobby.

Paradoxically, it is not a search for anything. What you think you are searching for will elude you because searching involves the mind. Surrender to your practice and whatever it brings. With surrender there is nothing to seek and nothing to expect. You serve your soul by surrendering to life. By trying to control what you think is life you are missing what life actually is. It is easy to make your body a tomb for the soul and your mind a prison for the sacred.

To complete the paradox, I give you the thoughts of the Spanish poet Antonio Machado (1875–1939). He observed that *no hay camino,* "there is no way," since the way is made by walking it. Machado counsels us not to have any preconceived notions about our journey but to be like the birds—they do not know about tomorrow, but they give themselves wholeheartedly to getting on with what has to be done today. Each human journey is unique, your journey is unique, just as the journey of all in creation is unique.

The great Native American Ponca shaman Standing Bear (ca. 1839–1908) remarked cryptically, "To walk the path to Light is a personal choice as well as a decision made between you and the Creator."

But this does not prevent you from traveling with a friend or companion; indeed, other benefits will come from the relationship—from the times when you work together, share your experiences, and support each other. However, if you prefer to be a solitary traveler, I am your spiritual friend.

In the practice of heart-centeredness, our pilgrimage is not so much a journey to travel, nor a hierarchical ladder to climb, but more like a circle to dance. For just as a rainbow shows all its colors at the same moment, the effect of heart-centeredness on the energy centers happens in all of them at the same moment to reveal that love has seven colors.

PART 1

*Opening to the
Inner Circle Teachings*

1

FROM CLOUDED
VISION TO
HEART-CENTEREDNESS

*Only your clouded vision prevents you from seeing that you
are all beings of light.*

THE HEALING WISDOM OF MARY MAGDALENE,
CHAPTER 2

THE INNER CIRCLE TEACHINGS are the teachings of spiritual
wisdom. This wisdom creates an opening to the reality of the spiritual
world. Spiritual wisdom is not a religion, nor is it about belief; it is a
revelation of the spiritual world.

At the core of spiritual wisdom is the soul, the individual expression
of Oneness, the Source. The soul is always present, at every moment,
at all times and in all situations. The mind, however, gives us a different message—one that leads to a sense of isolation, aloneness—and it
will constantly seek evidence to reinforce its message. Lack of awareness
of soul presence feeds the mind message. The Inner Circle Teachings
reveal that we are soul and soul is us—no isolation, no separation from
all that is sacred, for Oneness is All That Is. In each human being, the
place of the soul is the heart center, a subtle energy center and a superior

organ of perception. The Teachings show how this advanced form of perception is achieved through working with the heart center.

THE INNER CIRCLE TEACHINGS INTERPRETED FOR TODAY

Mary Magdalene and her soul mate Yeshua (Jesus) were spiritual masters who came to our planet bringing a simple yet profound message about who and what human beings are. To an inner circle of their closest followers, Yeshua and Mary Magdalene taught the core wisdom practice of the ancient mystery schools—the way of the heart (alluded to in Mark 4:33–34). In an interpretation for our times, *Love Has Seven Colors* presents the Inner Circle Teachings on heart-centeredness and explains how they positively affect the energetic processes of the subtle energy centers (Sanskrit: *chakra*). The ancient teachings stress that there is nothing that can be learned about them at the level of mind—where they remain as information; they can only be *experienced* at the level of the heart—where they become knowledge of the soul. To become heart centered is to be guided by your soul, the spiritual reality of your sacred self. The way forward demands that we commit to trying to become heart centered, and to keep on trying in spite of the overwhelming demands of our conditioned minds and the conditioned minds of others. This does not mean getting rid of the mind, or denying its reality; it means retraining the mind so that it can serve the soul. Together, soul and mind can manifest the sacred on the planet.

The simplicity of the Inner Circle Teachings is a mark of a universality that transcends any religion, cultural tradition, even time and place. With practice, your consciousness and awareness are enhanced as your ego-mind becomes progressively more aligned with your indwelling soul. An immediate outcome is that your whole being begins to open and expand. Putting the Teachings into practice will ultimately facilitate the desperately needed changes to the lives of the whole Earth Family and the planet that we all inhabit.

Today, in our own turbulent times, the call is heard again: the answer to our current dilemmas lies in the heart, the place of soul. Only our clouded vision prevents us from getting the perennial, universal message that we are all soul beings. Deep in our hearts we sense that this is so, as human beings down the centuries have sensed this inner knowing. The core elements of the Inner Circle Teachings can be summarized as follows:

- The concept of soul
- We are all spiritual beings
- Oneness
- Unconditional love
- Heart-centeredness
- The role of mind
- Clouded vision
- Healing
- The principal teachings of the seven centers

These concepts have found expression in various forms of religion and philosophical thought down through the ages.

Love Has Seven Colors teaches us how to become heart centered and how to practice heart-centeredness as a way of being. Heart-centeredness brings new and wise guidance on how to live from the perspective of unconditional love and compassion. With this new approach to being, positive, constructive energies flow out from you into the world, to other people and places. These changes happen because you are becoming more aligned with soul so that you, as an individual, become a vehicle for soul expression—a channel for the expression of unconditional love and Oneness in the world. You can influence what is without by realigning what is within.

THE RETURN OF THE FEMININE

Listening to your heart center for soul guidance is feminine wisdom. Interest in the powerful healing force of feminine wisdom has grown considerably in modern times. The return of the feminine to redress the disastrous imbalance in human life means the return of the soul in human consciousness. People reach out to the feminine—as goddess, as Mother Earth. These are signs of a need for reconnection with the soul. Movements motivated by elements of peace, caring, compassion, and concern for the Earth and the natural world are manifestations of this need. In this sense we are all suffering from the loss of the feminine and subsequent loss of soul.

The oppression of women and female children exactly parallels the dominance of conditioned masculine minds throughout most of history. Nevertheless, every effort to bring about female liberation in the truest sense has the energetic effect of opening the way for the liberation of the soul into human consciousness. When this happens, unconditional love will be brought to bear on all aspects of human and Earth Family life and our planet.

CLOUDED VISION

Clouded vision describes the way we perceive the world through the filter of our own conditioned minds. Learning how to access the heart center to perceive the world and to gain inner guidance is the process of removing clouded vision. The cloud is our conditioning: how we have perceived the world and how we have reacted to what we perceive. The cloud of conditioning determines the way we live our lives. Learning how to be heart centered offers the determined practitioner an opportunity to break free of this conditioning.

Recognizing Yourself as a Light Being

It would seem that one of the functions of creative people has been to hold on to the concept of soul and mourn the loss of soul consciousness. For example, over two hundred years ago, wandering in the rain-bathed countryside of the English Lake District, the poet William Wordsworth (1770–1850) was constantly inspired by his childhood discoveries in

Nature. The cycle of life and its progress through the seasons would bring to mind his own mortality, though such observations led him to consider the immortality of the soul. On such a day, a shard of light piercing the mist between the trees suddenly reminded him of magical times when he had been aware of the light emanating from everything he saw. That was then . . . way back. Had he dreamed it, he wondered? No, he could still remember. He took out his notebook to capture his memories in words. A few years later, with a mixture of nostalgia and joy, his published lines went,

> *There was a time*
> *When meadow, grove, and stream*
> *The earth and every common sight*
> *To me did seem*
> *Apparelled in celestial light*
> *The glory and freshness of a dream.*

Though in the same poem his sad reflection is, "The things which I have seen I now can see no more . . . Whither is fled the visionary gleam? Where is it now, the glory and the dream?" These are the heartfelt questions of someone who realizes that as the ego-mind develops and becomes conditioned, it becomes a kind of prison house in which we can forget who we are, even though "heaven lies about us in our infancy."

Happily, Wordsworth also reveals that, though his childhood visions faded, he was still aware that we are beings of light, souls incarnating into a physical body, so that "trailing clouds of glory do we come—from God, who is our home."

The Effects of Clouded Vision

Wordsworth, like so many people down the ages, seemed to understand that the cosmos, and especially planet Earth, exists as a physical place for soul to experience and express at this level of being. Since the physical matter of the cosmos is entirely composed of energy, we and every other physical thing emanate energy that can be perceived as light. Like Wordsworth, if we take a look at any infant we will see how they are absorbing the world around them, often staring wide-eyed, the light around people and things making them smile. Some infants stare at us with an unblinking gaze that seems to see right inside us. The conditioning that will come quite soon has not yet moved their consciousness out of the heart center.

As we grow and develop, the demands of parents and caregivers, society, education, and culture, the very environment in which we find ourselves, will all tend to challenge and change our perception of the world as a place of light and harmony. The glow that we once perceived begins to dim or disappear altogether. We inherit a world view of separateness and an approach to life and all we encounter that has to be processed through mind. This begins to lead to our sense of being apart from others, from everything outside of ourselves, and more seriously, from our instinctive soul being. Here, we find the answers to Wordsworth's poignant questions. We have developed clouded vision: the way that we perceive the world through the filter of the conditioned mind.

Yet, if we spend time in any natural setting, something seems to call to us. A beautiful view may evoke the call that we hear in the heart— the same call that the smile of a little infant sends out to us. Our vision may be clouded, but if we relearn how to listen, we can once again hear the quiet, calm voice of the heart.

ENTER THE SOUL

Earth is a unique destination for the journeying soul. Each of us embarks on an Earth life adventure that will be unique to us. We, the Earth, and the whole natural world are journeying together. Our mutuality suggests that our love for ourselves, each other, and the world around us should always be unconditional.

Our own creation begins outside of the physical level of space, time, and matter. It begins with the individuation of Oneness, referred to in this book as *soul,* the spiritual reality of each and every one of us. The soul exists before any physical life (incarnation), during physical life, and after the death of the body. Its purpose is to express the nature of Oneness through the medium of the physical cosmos. For a soul to incarnate and engage in the total experience of physicality, it needs an appropriate physical structure or vehicle. In our case this is a physical body. But the form that the physical body takes is determined by a range of factors, such as the parents, relevant environmental factors, and the process of birth. It needs to be recognized that the soul is unaffected by the form of the physical body that it will inhabit.

SOUL LOSS

Shamanic cultures around the world describe illness and disease as loss of soul. This is a metaphor for the soul's tendency to elude the grasp of everyday consciousness. The soul cannot be lost because it is always present, there is no "us" without soul. However, we do lose contact with its presence in our daily lives and this loss of relationship is reflected in bodily, mental, and emotional illness. Soul evades the mind that strives to control it. Mind has to be coaxed to let go of its need to be in control in order to experience what is beyond itself. Soul loss is the loss of connection with the sacred. Soul is "retrieved" when we become heart centered.

CONSCIOUSNESS AND THE
SUBTLE ENERGY SYSTEM

Your soul is connected to your body via the subtle energy system, especially through the seven main centers. We shall explore in depth the role that the soul plays in activating and maintaining heart-centeredness, and in enhancing the activities of each energy center—leading you to discover that love does indeed have seven colors!

When a person becomes heart centered, the soul is able to operate more easily and more powerfully through each of the energy centers, bringing a heightened awareness and sensibility that is transmitted to the personality consciousness. For example, Oneness can only be *experienced,* not understood by the mind. But when soul is able to operate more fully, we experience Oneness—we become conscious of total oneness with others, with animals and plants, with the environment, and with the rest of the planet. When this is the case, how different life will be for *all* of us.

We are witnesses to the fact that mind is no longer connected to the Source of Life, so that ego-mind consciousness has created a world where separation and patriarchy are the norm, bringing us to the chaotic times we know today. It seems that, in spite of what history clearly demonstrates, we are still unaware that this form of consciousness serves neither us nor the rest of the Earth Family. Our challenge is to realize that there is another, more powerful, consciousness waiting for us to embrace it: twenty-first-century consciousness. This is a consciousness of the heart, where the mind serves our soul's purpose, rather than the self-centered wants and desires of our conditioned personality, the ego. Heart-centered consciousness grows by listening to the guidance of the soul, and as it grows so our personality consciousness begins to merge with it. It is the new consciousness we need in order to build a more balanced world of peace and harmony for ourselves and each other, and for all those who follow after us.

As a newborn, we learned to breathe to begin our Earth journey. The pilgrimage to heart-centeredness requires that we relearn how to breathe and how to relax the physical body.

2
BREATH
AND RELAXATION

Our breathing should flow gracefully. To master your
breath is to be in control of your body and mind.

THICH NHAT HANH

WE BEGAN LIFE with the breath, the breath that has been the breath
of all life on Earth. The marvelous mystery of the universal breath is
that it unites our physical world with the world of spirit, and we will
always be part of it. Our breath connects us to All That Is. This enables
us to look at life from two perspectives: as a breathing individual and as
breathing Oneness. Both these realities are going on at the same time,
and breath carries us from one reality to the other. With every breath
we take, we are offered awareness of both realities.

This is why the very breathing moment contains all possibilities,
beyond just what is needed. Even though it may be prudent to look
ahead, even plan ahead, at certain times, if everything is considered
provisional, we can remain open to the event of the moment and allow
the future to flow into it.

CONSCIOUS BREATHING—
BREATHING WITH PURPOSE

Taking control of your breathing and your bodily relaxation sends a positive signal to your mind that you are in control. This in turn impacts on the mind's need to be constantly active and alert. The first preliminary exercise teaches you how to use the breath to totally relax, become calm, and develop serenity.

Pilgrimage Action 1

Full-Breath Breathing

This exercise reeducates your physical body about efficient energy breathing and thus maximizes your ability to take in available energies and expel energies that are no longer required. Full-breath breathing rebalances the whole system and realigns all aspects of your being. It can also be used as a self-healing activity to improve breathing capacity and rhythm. This will benefit your entire system. Once full-breath breathing becomes second nature you will find it easy to relax the body as well as your mind.

+ Sit comfortably in a chair, with your feet flat on the ground and your back straight. Raise your head until you can feel it aligned with your spine. Let your hands rest on your thighs or in your lap.
+ Notice your breathing. Notice what your chest and abdomen are doing. As you breathe in your normal, habitual way, which part of your body is moving the most? Allow your breathing to become slow, deep, and gentle.
+ In full-breath breathing, the focus is on the movement of the abdomen, rather than the chest. This is a big change to our usual way of breathing since we tend to be shallow breathers—moving the chest only.
+ Put your hands on your abdomen and imagine it is a balloon you are going to fill and then empty.

✦ As you slowly inhale through the nose, allow your "balloon" to fill by letting your abdomen gently expand, without any straining.

✦ Exhale slowly and feel the balloon of your abdomen deflate, without straining.

✦ Practice this exercise two more times, noting the difference between the in-breath and the out-breath, and how you feel as you breathe like this.

Full-breath breathing is also known as soft-belly breathing because it encourages the relaxation of the abdomen and discourages the tense, hard-belly approach to body posture. The soft-belly posture allows you to breathe deeply and gently so that you are calm and balanced, with your center of gravity below your navel. Awareness of your breath helps you become aware of where your thoughts come from, where they go, and what they might create. Full-breath breathing sends positive signals to the solar center, addressing the anxiety and fear stance of the ego-personality.

Remind yourself that your breath is part of the universal breath, breathed by all beings. Your breath connects with the air that you breathe and the winds that move across and surround the planet. This tells you that the sacred breath is not an ineffable, unreachable abstract concept of theology but is intimately bound up with our daily life of breath and breathing. Our breath will always carry us home.

CONSCIOUS RELAXATION

You may have noticed that you breathe at your best when your body is fully relaxed. All through the day there are times when we could benefit from being able to relax, really deeply, at a moment's notice. Conscious relaxation goes hand-in-hand with conscious breathing and both are necessary to access and maintain heart-centeredness.

Relaxation relieves tension and stress at all levels and allows the body's energies to flow more freely. The activities of the brain, heart, and lungs are slowed down, calming the mind and emotions. Calming our emotions and steadying the mind creates the ideal state for accessing the heart center. Developing a relationship with your relaxed physical body in this way also brings the benefits of reducing physical, emotional, and mental pain. Thus, you will also find it helpful, in so many ways, to be able to relax at will. You are now ready to use the power of conscious breathing to relax your body. The key to instant relaxation and calm is with the breath.

The next activity is a simple method of relaxing the whole body. In it you will send a command to your brain to allow all your muscles to relax, release, and let go of tension. You can facilitate this relaxation with slow, deep, and gentle breathing, which immediately sends positive messages to all the body systems. Everything is becoming calm and peaceful. Once your body and mind are acquainted with the feeling of relaxation, you will be able to move into relaxation mode at will.

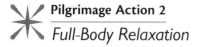 **Pilgrimage Action 2**
Full-Body Relaxation

The secret here is not to *try* to relax. Simply let go of tension each time you exhale. Since total relaxation can lead to sleep, try a sitting position to avoid this.

- ✦ In a sitting position in a comfortable chair, allow your legs to part slightly and let your hands rest lightly on your thighs.
- ✦ Take three full breaths, slowly and gently. Remember to let your soft belly breathe. As your mind presents problems or anxieties, let them go with your out-breath. Breathe them out through an open mouth. Close your mouth and breathe normally through your nose.
- ✦ Bring your focus to your hands. As you breathe in, clench them tightly to make a fist. As you breathe out, let them unclench. Repeat this. Breathe in and clench your fists. Let them unclench as you breathe out. Remember this feeling of unclenching and letting go as you exhale. This is how you relax.
- ✦ Do not clench anything again throughout the rest of this exercise. As you

breathe in, tell yourself that you are breathing in peace and relaxation. As you breathe out, know that you are relaxing and letting go.

✦ Move your attention to the back of your neck. Allow the in-breath to carry peace and relaxation to your neck. Relax and let go of the muscles of your neck as you exhale.

✦ Let that feeling of relaxation move down to your shoulders, then your arms and hands, using the out-breath to let go. Extend the feeling of relaxation to your chest and abdomen, letting go as you exhale. Relax and let go as you move down to the base of your spine.

✦ Allow the feeling of relaxation to move across your pelvis, then down into each leg as you relax and let go down to each foot. Continue to breathe slowly and gently.

✦ Staying relaxed, scan your body to check if any part has tensed up again. You will find that certain muscles may jerk or twitch as they get used to being relaxed.

✦ Take another breath during which you enjoy the sensation that the whole of your body is now relaxed. Enjoy the sensation of your relaxed body breathing. Notice how at the same time you are alert and aware. You are now in the perfect state to access your heart center.

MIND REACTS TO RELAXATION

A function of mind is to be alert, especially to change. This can interfere with breathing and relaxation. You will need to be prepared to be objective about mind's reactions to your intention. With practice it will become progressively easier to allow the flow of thoughts through your mind without your needing to grasp any of them. With practice, your mind begins to empty itself. This is an important outcome of combining relaxation with your breathing.

You can also practice this activity lying down. It is especially effective in encouraging rest or sleep. When this is your objective, you could spend more time relaxing your body, part by part, as you exhale.

Practice relaxation, or some form of it, so that it becomes second nature and you can do it anywhere, in any circumstance, in any position. Conscious relaxation, like conscious breathing, reestablishes a positive relationship with every aspect of your body.

THE LIFE FORCE

After feeling comfortable with relaxing your body, practicing full-breath breathing, and raising your awareness of the sacred nature of the breath, you should find that you have an increased facility within your body to receive and give out life energy. This is the life force, carried in the breath. The cycle of breathing is derived from the dual aspects of the energy cycle: inhalation is the receptive part of the cycle, while exhalation is the emissive part. Thus the life force has two complementary roles involving both aspects of the breathing and subtle energy cycle. This is the rhythm of the breath, a rhythm that is reflected throughout the natural world.

 Pilgrimage Action 3

Breathing and the Life Force

✦ As in the previous exercise, sit comfortably in a chair with your feet flat on the ground and your back straight. Raise your head until you can feel it aligned with your spine. Let your hands rest on your thighs or in your lap. Notice your breathing. Allow it to become slow, deep, and gentle.

✦ The life force comes to us in the breath. Be aware that you are breathing in the life force. Your blood system carries the life force to every cell in your body. This is an energizing force.

✦ As well as the life force, your breath carries oxygen, a vital component in maintaining your life. As you inhale, your lungs allow your blood system to transport oxygen to every cell in your body. Unused gases from your body's processes, especially carbon dioxide, are passed to the lungs for expulsion as you exhale. These gases are not wasted. They are life energy.

✦ Carbon dioxide is used by trees and plants for their respiration. One of the waste gases from their breathing process is oxygen. As you breathe in that oxygen, contemplate how the whole process of breathing is a cycle of interdependence between us and the plant world.

✦ Remember on your out-breath that your exhale serves the plant world, which also takes in the life force as the breathing spirit of all life.

✦ Remember on your in-breath that you are breathing in soul as the breathing spirit of all life.

✦ Breathe normally and gently, and sit with these elements of breathing for a while. Each inhalation is a new beginning. Inspiration comes from a steady breath.

Conscious breathing and full-body relaxation together send a powerful message to the three lower energy centers—base, sacral, and solar—processing the energies of physical humanness. All is well. This message is relayed via the heart center to the upper three centers—throat, brow, and crown—processing our spiritual humanness. The centers will be presented in the next chapter.

3

THE LIGHT BODY

Our God is Light. A day will come when you will understand what this means.

PIERRE BONNARD

THIS BOOK POSITS that we are souls with a physical body, not bodies with a soul. Soul first has contact with the physical energies of planet Earth through an energy field that may be envisaged as a body of light. Light, in this sense, refers to an energy frequency greatly beyond the speed of physical light, and is another term for *spirit,* the energy of the Source. For soul expression within the complete experience of physicality on Earth, the denser form of the physical body is needed. Soul's choice to incarnate into a physical body is about being human.

The light body is an energy field that surrounds each living thing. It is a complex, interwoven system composed of subtle layers that combine to represent the flowing energy, both physical and spiritual, that constitutes our being.

SUBTLE ENERGIES

Modern physics has at last discovered that there are energies that travel faster than the speed of light. Among these are the subtle energies of the light body and its transactions, and the spiritual energies that accompany the soul, including the life force. We all have the natural ability to detect subtle energies to a greater or lesser extent, generally using the ability unconsciously to ensure our survival. As you develop a new consciousness through working with your heart center, you will enhance this natural ability.

The Etheric Body

In the formation of the physical body of matter, soul first creates a subtle energetic structure that acts as a bridging level between the energetic level of soul, or spirit, and the very much denser level of physicality. This is the etheric body. This subtle structure is a system that will provide a template for the physical body as well as supporting its functions. The shape of the etheric structure is somewhat like that of the human body, having the appearance of being made of lines of light. Where lines converge or cross over, nodes of light are formed, the largest of which appear to be in line with the physical spine, with slightly smaller light nodes in the palms of the hands and the soles of the feet. As we follow any of the lines of light it can be seen that smaller nodes appear in conjunction with the skeleton and its joints, every organ of the body, and the bodily systems such as the vascular, digestive, and excretory systems. The total appearance of this energy field is like a galaxy of stars in the glowing shape of a human body.

The Emotional Subtle Body

Emotions are generated as energies when our positive or negative thoughts interact with physical life. These emotional energies vibrate at a far greater rate than the physical body, creating another energy body. In this energy body, our emotions and emotional reactions are processed. Feelings generated by the soul, acting as signals of warning, confirmation, or guidance, are also processed in this emotional level of our energy field.

The Mental Subtle Body

The mental functions of the mind create energies that travel at a far greater speed than light. Thought, will, and the power to drive

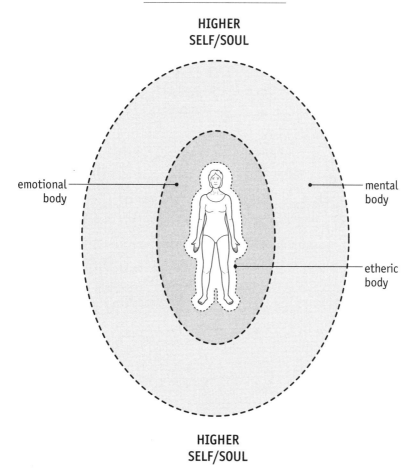

The light body—your energy field

thought into action vibrate at a far greater frequency than the physical body and the emotional subtle body. All thoughts, all actions, interactions, and reactions, are processed in this mental level of the energy field.

THE COMPLETE ENERGY FIELD—THE AURA

Our total energy field is the light body, the aura. It is made up of a series of energetic levels surrounding the physical. Their vibratory frequency increases from the physical, up through the etheric, the emotional, and mental bodies, to the soul. The different rates of vibration between the energetic levels allow them to be interpenetrating rather than simply fitting one inside the other. The various vibrating energies that surround the physical body create an energy field around each person that, appearing to subtle vision as a vast bubble of light, has been described since ancient times as the aura (from Greek, *avra*). This phenomenon has been known by indigenous cultures worldwide for thousands of years. The energy field is the "celestial light" that Wordsworth saw as a child. Many people today can also testify to having the same experience as a small child. One's energy field contains evidence of the soul's journey in its embodied form on Earth. Working with the heart center will enable you to detect this energetic material and become aware of the energetic transactions in your own field as well as those of others, those of animals and plants, even landscape elements, and in the universal energy field that surrounds us.

THE EGO-MIND

Once the physical body is established, the mind enables a person to be conscious of the physical state and to develop a consciousness of themselves as individuals (ego). This indicates to the developing person that they are separate from every other person and every other thing in its environment. These perceptions encourage the ego-mind to create a strong tendency toward personal survival and personal advancement. This sense of separation eventually overshadows the fact that we are souls with a body, not bodies with a soul.

Over time, through this developmental process, human beings have created a world dominated by the wants and desires of individual minds. The reason why we incarnated on the physical level of being is totally ignored or obscured. The ego-mind operates as if soul reality is a threat to its very existence. This state of affairs has led us to the plight of our world, with its divisions, injustices, pain, and unhappiness.

THE ENERGY FIELD AT WORK

The light body regulates the amount and quality of energy to which we are exposed by only allowing the absorption of energies compatible with our own. Energetic compatibility depends on our level of consciousness and can vary from moment to moment. But the light body can accumulate what Andean shamans call "heavy" or dark energy. If heavy energy is allowed to build up, it will affect the subtle energy system. The effects of build-up are then conveyed to the physical body. Eventually, through symptoms of distress, discomfort, or even illness, the body warns us that we need to do something about the accumulation of heavy energy. This is why we should clear the energy field of negative energies from time to time. The clearing activity, described in Pilgrimage Action 7 (pages 45–46), is one of the empowering tools for clearing your system. Prayer and meditation also help to release heavy energy. These are all tools that can clear the way for finer energies to enter your energy field.

Energetic harmony ensures that we maintain our well-being and develop a fluid consciousness that allows us to embrace, and flow through, the unpredictability and uncertainty presented by change. Conscious fluidity is a state of alertness and awareness that allows us to recognize opportunities and take risks that encourage spiritual growth for both ourselves and our community.

THE ETHERIC BODY— THE SUBTLE ENERGY CENTERS

The seven main energy centers are located in the etheric body. They are, effectively, levels of consciousness acting as portals into our life journey, our health, and well-being. Their function is to allow the flow of energy to and from the various levels of our being and to process the energies generated by specific life issues. For these reasons you should not attempt to shut off their activity by fully closing them. The seven main energy centers of the etheric body are connected to a central channel aligned with the spine.

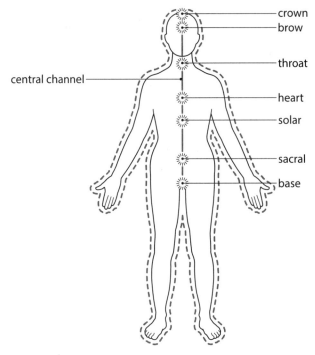

crown
brow

throat

central channel

heart
solar

sacral
base

The seven main energy centers of the etheric body

When a center is activated, its appearance as a vortex of light changes as it moves out from the surface of the etheric body to project into the energy field. It now appears as a bell- or funnel-shaped structure, connected at its narrower end to the central channel. This shape facilitates the gathering in, or radiating out, of energies. Even as specific processes are taking place in each center, the system operates as an interconnected whole, with each center aware of the activities of all the other centers in the system. The centers are subtle energetic structures whose energies link with the physical body through the relevant endocrine glands in the physical body. An outline of the functions of the centers follows.

The Base Center

The base center roots us into the physical, grounds us to physical life, and attaches us to planet Earth. Located in the etheric body, opposite the base of the spine, this center processes all issues of a physical nature: how we each relate to our body and its physicality, our senses, sensuality, our sex or gender, our safety and survival, self-defense and aggression, our relationship to all aspects of the natural world, and our relationship to the planet. These issues are all related to our basic human nature.

The base center is linked to the body via the adrenal glands, which are situated on top of the kidneys. These glands initiate physical action, especially the fight-or-flight response that is part of our self-defense system. This center is also concerned with the base of the spine, the lower pelvis and related organs, the hips, legs, and feet. It is the keeper of cellular memory for the whole physical body.

The base center has a special link with the heart and crown centers. This link gives a strong clue about our reality. The base center emphasizes that we are in a physical body in a physical world, but our true nature is soul, signified by the heart center, and our origins are spiritual, signified by the crown center.

Each center color is at its brightest when the center is in a state of balance. The colors may be seen with subtle vision and are similar, but not identical, to the colors of the rainbow. Balance occurs when a person feels safe and secure and has a good relationship with the body and the natural world. When in a state of balance, the base center vibrates to the color red. This is the first color of our human rainbow.

The Sacral Center

Located in the etheric body, opposite the sacral bones in the spine, between the navel and the base center, the sacral center processes all issues of creativity and sexuality. This center keeps a subtle energetic record of our development from birth and is the safe, happy home of the human child. However, when a person has experienced childhood trauma, the energy pattern known as the damaged inner child is often found misplaced in either the base center (physical trauma) or solar center (emotional or mental trauma).

The sacral center is the seat of joy, which is not simply an emotion but an energy generated in this center, telling us that we are in touch with the center's spiritual aspects. This is often expressed in the form of giggly laughter, especially in children. Being human allows us creative potential as a natural manifestation of our unique spirituality. But suppression of creativity or sexuality creates issues that have to be processed by this center. There is a useful question to ask when we need to assess how we really feel about something: Does it give me joy?

The sacral center links with the body via the sex glands (the testes in the male or the ovaries in the female). It is concerned with the urogenital organs, the uterus (womb), the kidneys, the lower digestive organs, and the lower back. Males should realize that though they may not have a physical uterus, they do have a sacral center that acts like one. All creations have their beginnings and gestation here.

Our creativity, sexuality, and our feelings of joy are linked to our identity, so that if we are unable to properly express these aspects of self, the center moves out of balance and begins to find ways to signal this. The sacral center has a special link with the throat center, where the life issues that the sacral center processes are given expression. When in a state of balance, the sacral center vibrates to the color orange, the second color of our human rainbow.

The Solar Center and the Mind

The solar center is located in the etheric body, opposite the nerve junction known as the solar plexus. This is below the breastbone and the diaphragm, and above the navel. The nerves of this plexus radiate out like the rays of the sun and echo their subtle activity pattern in the center. The solar center links with the body via the Islets of Langerhans, the endocrine glands in the pancreas. The energies of the solar center affect the digestive system, the pancreas, the liver and gallbladder, the middle back, and the band of muscle at the base of the chest, the diaphragm. Since breathing rhythm is governed by the movement of the diaphragm, the processing of solar center energies is directly linked to our breathing.

Our thoughts, emotions, and feelings, as well as our sense of personal self and personal power, are processed by this center. Here we discover how far life experience has empowered or disempowered us and how we react to people and situations in terms of our sense of self. As we have grown, developed, experienced life, and reacted to the behavior of others, our sense of self has been created by our mind, making our personality a conditioned being. The unconditioned being that watches over us at all times, without any kind of judgment, is our soul.

The mind alerts us to problems, even when these are imagined or of our own making. So the mind can generate feelings of fear and alarm that can, in turn, affect our emotional state. All such energies are processed by the solar center so that they then have a direct influence on the movement of the diaphragm. We sense the early stages of this influence as nervous feelings like butterflies in the stomach, followed by interrupted or constricted breathing. In its extreme form, interrupted diaphragm movement can lead to hyperventilation or even a cessation of breathing. The way to counteract the effect of the mind's fears is through conscious control of the breath.

The solar center confronts us with all issues connected to the mind—our thoughts and emotions, and especially our conditioned mind-sets. The mind is designed to record and remember, and this process begins in, and continues from, our time in the womb. Since some of our experience will inevitably seem to be negative, we find that not all of the mind's conditioning is conducive to our well-being. The solar center allows us to store mental and emotional patterns of energy that, because they have not been fully processed, can trigger reactions we would rather not experience. When this occurs, we are in danger of moving into a state of energetic imbalance and our feelings tell us how uncomfortable this is.

Being aware of our triggered reactions is important when considering the solar center's link with the brow center. Though the solar center processes mental activity, it has access to intuitive information through its link with the brow center. This level of information is generally the wisdom of the soul. Thus we are able to compare and contrast these two related forms of information. And yet so often we listen to the overriding voice of the mind. For example, have you ever had an idea about something, and it seems like a good idea, but then you start to think it over? You end up changing your mind, only to find later that your first impulse was the best one.

We become conditioned by the rationality of the mind to trust its findings and messages above all else. What we need to remember is that the mind can only work with what it already knows, with what is in the memory bank. Material from the brow is always fresh and often unknown, so that when the mind is confronted with such material, it tends to challenge it.

Through the interactions of this center, we discover much about our emotions and the workings of the mind, their effects on breathing, and our feelings of well-being. The solar center provides the gateway to being able to understand and witness how conscious breathing can positively change these effects. It is here that conscious breathing reveals clues to personal empowerment, for as we shall see, it is conscious breathing that we will use to access soul and soul guidance via the heart center.

In its balanced state, the solar center vibrates to the color golden yellow, the third color of our human rainbow.

The Heart Center

The heart center is the place of soul. Located in the etheric body at the center of the chest—not in the *physical* heart—the heart center is where the soul can be accessed. The challenge of the heart center is to express the light of the soul as love, to convey its soul message of love through to us, and to deal with all issues about love, and the absence of love, in our life.

The heart center links with the body via the thymus gland, the gland that is partially responsible for the development of the immune system. Issues around love and the absence of love affect our immune system throughout life. The processing of such issues by the heart center will often manifest in the physical body as various diseases related to the immune system. The signal is that we need to address the issues in question.

The cardiac and pulmonary nerve plexuses, the heart, lungs, the bronchial tubes, chest, upper back, and arms are all influenced by the heart center. Similarly, information about what happens to these organs passes to other levels of our being via this center.

The body has four main systems for distributing and circulating both the physical and energetic products of life. These are the nervous system, the endocrine glands with their links to the seven main energy centers, the subtle energy system, and the blood (vascular) system. Understood by most ancient cultures as both sacred and mysterious, blood carries the life force (entering via the breath) and the physical and energetic products of the other three systems. The physical heart acts as the distributor for the blood system. Thus all the energies of life, both physical and subtle, pass through it and on into the heart energy center.

The heart center is at the balance point of the seven main centers, so that balance is one of its important functions. The center has to balance the energies moving upward from the base center toward the brow with the spiritual energies moving downward from the crown center. In all cases, the heart center monitors how much the conditioned personality is involved and how much the soul is involved, and is constantly seeking to create a balance between them.

We are living in a time when this balance point of the centers, is also the crisis point in human affairs. If you think back, you will find that some issue around love has been your greatest life challenge so far. You are not alone. It will continue to be so for all people on the planet. Via the heart center, the soul/Self asks, Do you love yourself, and do you love others? Do you love others because of Oneness, and can you love without judgment? Your heart knows and cannot be fooled.

But these questions are also about whether we are at last willing to move from a fear-based to a love-based way of being. The fear-based way keeps us in the solar center, in the grip of the conditioned mind. We know what fear would do—fear trusts power and violence. After all, there is plenty of evidence to prove this. We have had thousands of years of trying to solve all our problems this way, and we go on with this way in spite of the evidence that it has never provided a long-term solution. This is why the challenge of our times is to move our consciousness out of the solar center and into the heart center. Then we can ask, What would *Love* do? Love will give an answer to any problem, on any occasion. For when the heart is asked, the soul replies and shows us the way through with Love's answer. Love's answer makes everybody happy and everybody wins.

When in a state of balance, the heart center vibrates to the color green, the color of balance. It is not surprising that, when we recognize the need to revive and refresh ourselves, we go somewhere in nature, unconsciously seeking the energies of the color green, the fourth color of our human rainbow.

The Throat Center

Located in the etheric body opposite the throat and affecting its related organs, the throat center is the "ear, nose, and throat" center too. It links with the body and these organs via the thyroid gland. As mentioned earlier, the throat has an important energetic link with the sacral center, where everything creative is conceived and gestated. The throat center processes issues of expression and communication, and all the different methods we use to express ourselves and communicate with others and with the world, as well as with the realms of the sacred.

In the other centers it may take time before we are aware of a block in the flow of energies in the system. However, if we suppress the expression of any of the issues dealt with by the throat center, we may feel a pain in the throat or the need to cough, straight away.

When in a state of balance, the throat center vibrates to the color sky blue. Often the color of healing energies as perceived by subtle sensing, this is the fifth color of our human rainbow.

The Brow Center

Located in the etheric body opposite the middle of the forehead, just above the brow, the brow center links with the body via the pituitary gland and hypothalamus in the brain. It is concerned with the brain, eyes, and face. One of the roles of the brow center is to oversee the operation of all the centers below it. When subtle energies arrive here for transmission to the crown, the brow will send them back down the system if they have not been processed because we have not dealt with the relevant issues. The brow center also controls energy moving down from the crown center. It will not pass this energy down through the system if the centers are not receptive.

An illustration of how the physical body is based on the light body template is the way the pituitary gland and hypothalamus mirror the overseeing activities of the brow center by controlling and monitoring the secretions of all the other endocrine glands.

The brow center processes information from our psychic awareness or subtle sensing—our so-called sixth sense—as well as information from our intuitive awareness. Both forms of energetic information are passed to the solar center, via its special link with the brow. Here, energetic information very often clashes with our mental attempts to understand it.

Psychic awareness enables us to be aware of subtle energetic phenomena, such as the light of the energy field around someone. It is the awareness that tells us when we enter a room, for example, that people have just had an argument. We actually pick up the vibrations of this happening before we even see their faces. The fabric of a building absorbs energy so that, in the same way, psychic awareness enables a sensitive person to become aware of past events that may have happened in that building. These energies are external to us. On the other hand, intuitive awareness enables us to be aware of messages from the soul and of information from the spiritual levels—energies that are internal.

Our problem with all of the input to and from the brow center is that once it is conveyed to the brain for interpretation, the mind steps in to act as uninvited consultant. But the mind is only able to compare information received with what it already knows and understands. If the conditioned mind cannot match the information with our perceived life experience, it tends to put that information straight in the discard tray. This strengthens the mind so that it can develop an immediate reject reaction to spiritual experiences and information.

Since ancient times the brow center has been called the third eye, because a way of seeing beyond the ordinary or the appearance of things seems to originate here. This is exactly what the brow center can do in terms of both our psychic and intuitive awareness. Indeed, life is enhanced when we learn to use and trust these natural psychic abilities. The practice of working with the heart center greatly enhances these abilities when we begin to sense with the "eyes of the soul."

When balanced, the brow center vibrates to a deep royal blue or indigo light, the sixth color of our human rainbow.

The Crown Center

Located in the etheric body above the crown of the head, this center deals with issues of our spirituality. It challenges us to acknowledge the spiritual truth of being and to allow this to be fully expressed in our lives.

The crown center links with the body via the pineal gland, which tells us about the amount of sunlight we are getting and whether we are getting enough. This gland also mirrors the crown center's role of telling us about the amount of spiritual light we are allowing into our life and whether this is enough. When we do not get enough sunlight, as those who live in gray climates well know, we feel depressed. If deprivation goes on long enough, this can become the medical condition known as seasonal affective disorder (SAD syndrome). The remedy is to get some sunlight as soon as possible. Deep depression or despair can be seen as a symptom of lack of spiritual light. This is why many cultures see such states as a disease of the spirit, a disease that should be tackled immediately. The remedy, of course, is a good dose of spiritual light.

The special energetic link between the crown and base centers tells us that life is not about being either spiritual or human, but both. Life is a sacred journey, a spiritual event, and we and all other beings are an expression of the one Source. The indigenous Lakota (or Sioux) people of North America proclaim this idea during any sacred act or ceremony when they pray—*Mitakuye oyasin!* (We are all related.) Just as the base center ensures our grounding in physical life, so the crown center maintains our link with the sacred and our true identity as spiritual beings.

When we are living this expression of Oneness, the crown center vibrates to the color violet, the seventh color of our human rainbow.

THE ETHERIC BODY—THE HUMAN RAINBOW

At a subtle level, our energy centers give us the appearance of walking rainbows. All the center colors are needed to make a rainbow, and the fact that our energy centers vibrate to the colors of the rainbow tells us that our life is, and always was, a complete whole. There is no issue or experience that does not have a valid place in our unique story. With this in mind, it is helpful to recall the functions of the seven main centers in relation to our total being as souls having a human experience.

The lower three energy centers, via the mind, exert a pressure on our personality to engage in physicality and every aspect of human life. Consequently, the personality may well, and often does, interpret its view of human life as all there is. The mind then tells us that there are plenty of logical and scientific arguments to support this view. The energies moving upward from the lower three centers enter the heart center where they will be assessed to see how much they have been associated with unconditional love. At the same time, the upper three centers of the crown, brow, and throat, via our intuition and feelings, exert a "downward" pressure on the personality to recall our Light, or spiritual, origins. In this way the heart center has to deal with the energetic traffic of all the centers. When this energy flow is concerned with stresses in any, some, or all of the centers, the consequent tension may have a negative effect on the physical heart.

The heart center shows us that we will only ever be half of what we can be until we take a leap of faith and trust in our reality as soul beings. Through its processing of life issues, the heart center shows us that unconditional love is the key to a harmonious balance of both the physical and spiritual aspects of our being. Here, love is a state of being and that state is devoid of fear. The opposite of love is fear. Hate is one of the many by-products of fear. The Source/God is love, yes, but this is an unconditional love beyond the imagination of the mind. This love is the primordial energy of the cosmos, the life force in the breath of life, the interbreathing spirit of all life.

4

GETTING TO KNOW YOUR
ENERGY CENTERS

Energy is an eternal delight.

WILLIAM BLAKE

YOU CAN NOW USE your conscious breathing and your ability to relax to sense the position of your energy centers in relation to your physical body. Recall the relative position of the energy centers, as set out in the previous chapter. They are subtle energetic, not physical, structures, so that during each activity you will sense them first in your energy field and then as a sensation in an area of your body.

The next activity is about locating the seven main energy centers that are aligned with your spine. The activity encourages you to sense that each center emits a different energy and notice how your sensations may change according to what a particular center is processing.

✳ Pilgrimage Action 4
Sensing the Position of the Energy Centers

As mentioned earlier, when practicing any of the Pilgrimage Actions for the first time it may be helpful to have someone read them out to you. If no one is available, make a recording of yourself reading them.

✦ Stand with both feet flat on the ground with your arms by your sides. Or you can sit comfortably on a chair with your legs and arms uncrossed (if they remain crossed there is an energy block at the point of crossover), and your feet flat on the ground, with your hands resting on the thighs. Relax and breathe normally.

✦ Use your breath to help you stay relaxed as your mind starts to collate the subtle energy information that you are sensing.

✦ Rub your palms together to sensitize them. The activity begins at the crown center, at the top of your head and more or less in line with the spine. Raise your hands up so that your palms can be held above your crown center with your arms fully extended. Keep a small gap between your hands.

✦ Slowly lower your arms, allowing your palms to move down toward your crown center until you sense a slight pressure or resistance against your palms, or a tingling in them. Stop at this point. Notice the position of the center and your sensations.

✦ This is the edge of the radiation you can sense from the crown center. Notice how the crown center energies extend upward into the energy field.

✦ Now you are going to sense the location of your brow center. Here, the energies project in front of and behind the center but you will only be able to sense those projecting out in front of you. Move your hands in front of your forehead with your arms extended as much as you can.

✦ Slowly bring both your palms in toward your brow center until you sense the slight pressure of its projected energies. Notice the position of the center and any sensations. Stop at this point and notice where the brow energies extend into your energy field. Notice any differences in sensation between your brow and crown centers.

✦ Move both your hands down to the throat area. Again, extend your palms away from the throat area and slowly bring them toward the throat center. Notice the position of the center and your sensations. Do you experience a difference in sensation between your throat and brow centers?

✦ Move both hands down in front of the middle of your chest, with your arms extended. Slowly bring your palms toward the middle of your chest to locate the heart center. Again, notice the position of the center and your sensations. Do you experience a difference in sensation between your heart and throat centers?

✦ Keep your palms over your heart center for a few moments. The Teachings stress that you will be working with this center from now on.

✦ Move both hands down to just below and in front of your breastbone and diaphragm, above the navel. Keep both arms extended. Slowly bring them toward your body, and with your palms locate the solar center. Notice the position of the center and your sensations. How does this energy differ from what you experienced in the throat?

✦ Move both hands just below your navel. Keep both arms extended. Slowly bring them in toward your abdomen, and with your palms locate the sacral center. Notice the position of the center and your sensations. How does this energy differ from the solar center?

✦ Finally, move your hands to position them in front of the base center, at the base of your spine. When you are in a sitting position, the base center energies project upward in the front of the body and downward at an angle of about forty-five degrees to the base of the spine.

✦ Proceed in the same way as for the other centers to sense the energies of the base center as they project outward. Notice the position of the center and your sensations. How does this energy differ from the sacral center?

✦ With your focus in the base center, ground yourself by sensing your feet in touch with the Earth.

✦ Relax and consider where you have located your centers and what you have discovered about the energies they emit.

This activity can be repeated to enable you to become more familiar with locating your energy centers.

THE ENERGY CENTERS
OF THE HANDS AND FEET

Two of the seven main energy centers have links with centers in the hands and feet. Those in the hands are linked to the heart center. Those in the feet are linked to the base center. As well as processing the specific energies mentioned below, these links mean that our hands and feet are connected to all the other centers and their subtle and physical life processes. Traditional Chinese medicine and acupuncture give us clues about the functions of these four important centers.

The Palm Centers

In traditional Chinese medicine, the *laogong* acupuncture point on the palm of the hand is related to the heart, blood circulation, and the release of negative *qi,* or heavy energy. This tells us about the vital energetic link between the centers of the two palms and the heart. The heart center is the key to the subtle aspects of the breath and healing and the link means that the palms of each hand can act as extensions of the heart in conveying love and healing. Hence we can soothe, touch, caress, and care for others with the hands. However, when the hands are used to hurt another there is a negative effect on the heart center and our breathing rhythm. Try the next activity to sense the hand–heart link.

✳ Pilgrimage Action 5
Sensing the Hand–Heart Energy Link

This action will extend the sensitivity you have discovered through the activities you have practiced so far. The first part focuses on drawing in energy, the second on giving it out.

+ Sit in a chair in a relaxed position with your legs uncrossed and your feet flat on the floor. Hold your palms out, facing away from you, with your arms bent at the elbow. Relax your elbows, the back of the neck, and the shoulders. Close your eyes if this helps your concentration. Breathe normally.

✦ Focus your attention on the palm centers. As you inhale, imagine that you are drawing energy in through the palm centers. Breathe out gently, focusing through your palms. Note your sensations.

✦ Now visualize the energetic link between your palms and your heart center. Breathe in and sense energy moving up your arms, across your shoulders, to converge in the heart center in the middle of your chest.

✦ Lower your arms and relax for a few moments. Raise your arms again, with your hands held out in front of you as before. In this second part of the activity you are going to send energy from your heart center to the palms.

✦ Put your attention in your heart center and relax. Breathe into the center. As you exhale, visualize energy moving from your heart center, across your shoulders, down the arms, to the center in each palm. Send this energy out to who or what comes into your mind.

Compare your experiences of absorbing and transmitting energy via your palm and heart centers, and make a note of the sensations in your journal.

The Sole-of-the Foot Centers

Linked energetically with the base center, the energy centers in the soles of the feet absorb energies from the Earth. The base center and the sole-of-the-foot centers act as grounding points for incoming subtle energies. These life-giving energies are essential to the physical body and physical life. This is why it is good to walk barefoot whenever you can, a practice that will lead to the pleasure of sensing the Earth in a deeper way. Take every opportunity to walk barefoot when safe to do so.

In traditional Chinese medicine, the *yongquan* acupuncture point on the sole of the foot is connected to the kidneys and is a focus for treatment in cases of hypertension. This acupuncture point is in the same place as the sole-of-the-foot energy center (just behind the middle of the two large pads at the front of the foot). Its function describes the link between the centers of the feet and the base center, because base center energies are transmitted to the body via the adrenal glands. These glands, situated at the top of the kidneys, secrete hormones associated with the bodily states of hypertension, stress, or anxiety. The next activity helps you sense with your sole-of-the-foot centers.

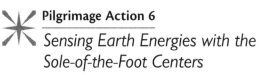

Pilgrimage Action 6

Sensing Earth Energies with the Sole-of-the-Foot Centers

+ If possible, stand on the ground with bare feet. Take up a relaxed posture with your feet a shoulder-width apart. Take six slow, full breaths, then breathe normally.

+ Pay attention to the soles of your feet. Be aware of your contact with the Earth, as well as with the ground under your feet. Close your eyes and notice whether you can sense an energetic flow via the soles of your feet.

+ Still with your focus in the feet, use the in-breath to aid your awareness of the passage of energy from the ground into your feet, up your legs to the base center. Inhale a few times with this intention.

Note your discoveries in your journal. Experiment. Repeat the exercise in different locations and at different times of the day. What did you discover?

Your experiences with the two previous activities should reinforce your understanding of the role of the hands and feet in absorbing subtle energy and how this is enhanced by conscious breathing. The sole centers, through their contact with the planet, keep our energetic activity grounded. Grounding ourselves is important for our efficient functioning as a channel for healing and other energies, and for channeling these to others. Through the palm centers we transmit subtle energies and absorb energetic information. During this activity, the centers enable us to perceive or sense the movement of subtle energies. Developing sensitive palm centers will give you new insight into the functioning of your heart center and its role in hands-on healing.

Via the activities described above, you can use the centers in your feet to make conscious contact with the Earth, and the centers in your hands to make conscious contact with your heart. These two sets of energy centers provide us with an opportunity to celebrate our love for the Earth, perhaps through dance and movement, and our love for others and the Earth Family, perhaps through using the hands to heal, comfort, prepare food, make music, and the like.

PROTECTING YOUR ENERGY FIELD

Now that you are familiar with the location of your energy centers, at this point you need to remember that it is essential to look after yourself and your energy field. If you wish to follow another exercise, or some other spiritual practice such as meditation, you are in the ideal state to do this. If not, you should be aware that your efforts have opened your energy centers more than is needed for everyday functioning and you no longer need to be open to that level of energy flow. You can reduce that advanced state of openness. This can be done by carrying out the three following activities.

When linked as one procedure, these three activities realign your centers and protect your energy field. This is particularly necessary if you are going to expose yourself to other situations, such as the routine supermarket trip, where you would be too open to external energies. Regulating your energy centers helps ensure sound sleep. It means returning your subtle energy system to everyday functioning. It is linked to closing your practice sessions. It does not, however, mean fully closing the energy centers or shutting down any of the body systems.

✳ Pilgrimage Action 7
Clearing Your Energy Field

+ If possible, stand with your feet a shoulder-width apart and your arms hanging loosely by your sides. Gently flex the knees and allow your body to relax.

✦ Take a moment to be aware of any heavy energy in your body and energy field, noting where it seems to have accumulated. (It is worth making a note of this observation in your journal every time you do this exercise to see if there is a pattern.)

✦ Now visualize yourself under a shower or gentle waterfall of silver light. Breathe in. As you exhale, let this light pour over you, through you, and out into your surrounding field, especially to any place where you sensed an accumulation of heavy energy. Allow the silver light to exit through your hands and feet, and every orifice of the body.

✦ Notice the color of the light that moves in to fill the space that you have cleared. Your awareness of this color will confirm that the clearing is taking place. You might sense this in a number of ways. If you feel you are sensing nothing (it is your mind saying you can't), carry out this important exercise as if you can.

✦ Note the sensations of clearing and the sensations of being cleansed.

CLEARING NEGATIVE THOUGHTS

All thought is a form of energy and an energetic law is that like tends to attract like. Negative thoughts do just this—they attract more negative thoughts. This is why, when we feel despondent or depressed, if we are unable to control our thoughts or thinking patterns we may soon feel worse as more negative thoughts pour into the mind to reinforce our unhappy feelings. The mind then stores this material. An antidote to this unhelpful process is to clear negative thought energy.

Using the previous Pilgrimage Action whenever it feels necessary, you can clear yourself of conditioned mind negativity—about yourself, others, the state of the world, what you are doing, what you have done, what you are yet to do. Something that you need to let go of will come to mind as you read this.

You will have noticed how open your energy centers can be. In the next activity, you bring your energy centers from being wide-open back to everyday functioning.

✳ Pilgrimage Action 8
Regulating Your Energy Centers

Since your energy centers have a three-dimensional structure, you will find it helpful to visualize them as colored flowers with petals that are able to close up, but not shut tightly. See the colors as light. Your intention is to reduce the advanced state of energetic openness and bring the centers to everyday functioning.

✦ Still standing relaxed, with knees gently flexed, put your mind in your crown center. Visualize the flower of your crown center having the color violet. Breathe in. As you exhale, visualize the petals of your crown center flower closing up a little.

✦ Move your awareness to the brow center, color indigo or royal blue. Breathe in. As you exhale, visualize the center's petals closing up a little.

✦ Move your awareness to the throat center, color sky blue. Breathe in. As you exhale, visualize the center's petals closing up a little.

✦ Move your awareness to the heart center, color green. As you exhale, visualize the center's petals closing up a little.

✦ Move your awareness to the solar center, color golden yellow. As you exhale, visualize the center's petals closing up a little.

✦ Move your awareness to the sacral center, color orange. As you exhale, visualize the center's petals closing up a little.

✦ Move your awareness to the base center, color glowing red. As you exhale, visualize the center's petals closing up a little.

✦ Now notice the first color that comes to mind. This is the color of energy that will keep your system in place. Breathe in and, as you exhale, surround yourself with a sphere of this colored light.

This is also a grounding process. Note the direction of activity: from the highest vibration of the crown center to that closest to the Earth at the base center.

The third activity keeps your energy field strong and protects you by not allowing the entry of incompatible energies.

Pilgrimage Action 9
The Sphere of Protection

✦ Still standing relaxed and breathing naturally, breathe in and visualize the sphere of light around you. As you exhale, surround the sphere of light around you with a sphere of golden light. See this golden sphere sparkle and gleam. This will tell you about its energy of strength and protection. Before moving back into your everyday consciousness, enjoy the sensation of being in this light.

✦ Remember to coordinate your visualization with your out-breath. Whenever it feels necessary, you can visualize the Sphere of Protection around yourself.

Once you have learned them, the three Pilgrimage Actions above can be practiced as one complete activity.

Now that you are familiar with your energy centers, the next activity will help you maintain a vibrant relationship with them.

Pilgrimage Action 10
Balancing the Rainbow

This activity balances each of the energy centers with color visualization and relevant affirmations. It may also be practiced as a meditation on the centers. It can be very helpful to practice this activity with a pilgrim partner who can talk you through each stage. First, make sure that you know the relative position of each of your energy centers.

✦ Sit or stand comfortably. Use your breathing to relax your body. As you breathe and relax, close your eyes and visualize your light body surrounding you as an aura of shimmering light.

✦ Imagine that you are in a beautiful natural setting. It has been raining and the rain has just stopped. The rainfall leaves you feeling cool and refreshed. You breathe out with a feeling of satisfaction.

✦ You look into the distance and see a rainbow in which the colors are vivid. You go toward the rainbow until you can see each color quite clearly. Keep your eyes closed to aid your inner vision.

✦ Put your hand on your heart center. Looking at the rainbow, choose the red color that you feel you need. Breathe this color into your base center. As you breathe, say mentally or out loud, "I honor the Earth and the Earth Family." Pause to allow this statement to be absorbed into your base center.

✦ Move your attention to your sacral center. From the rainbow, choose the orange color that you feel you need. Breathe this color into your sacral center. As you breathe, say mentally or out loud, "I honor my body and my sexuality." Pause to allow this statement to be absorbed into your sacral center.

✦ Move your attention to your solar center. From the rainbow, choose the golden-yellow color that you feel you need. Breathe this color into your solar center. As you breathe, say mentally or out loud, "I honor my mind." Pause to allow this statement to be absorbed into your solar center.

✦ Move your attention to your heart center. From the rainbow, choose the green color that you feel you need. Breathe this color into your heart center. As you breathe, say mentally or out loud, "I honor my sacred self." Pause to allow this statement to be absorbed into your heart center.

✦ Move your attention to your throat center. From the rainbow, choose the sky-blue color that you feel you need. Breathe this color into your throat center. As you breathe, say mentally or out loud, "I honor my truth." Pause to allow this statement to be absorbed into your throat center.

✦ Move your attention to your brow center. From the rainbow, choose the indigo/royal-blue color that you feel you need. Breathe this color into your brow center. As you breathe, say mentally or out loud, "I honor my inner vision." Pause to allow this statement to be absorbed into your brow center.

✦ Move your attention to your crown center. From the rainbow, choose the violet color that you feel you need. Breathe this color into your crown center. As you breathe, say mentally or out loud, "I am one with All That Is." Pause to allow this statement to be absorbed into your crown center.

✦ Now visualize your energy field, vibrating with rainbow colors, swirling around you. Breathe in any colors that seem to catch your attention.

✦ Now see a golden light of protection around you as each center returns to an everyday level of activity.

You can practice this activity at your own pace, perhaps spending different amounts of time at each center while the balancing process takes place.

The need for balance in the subtle energy system brings us to the two complementary subtle energy channels that support the etheric body. They are the subject of the next chapter.

5

DUALITY AND POLARITY

People desire to separate their worlds into polarities of dark
and light, ugly and beautiful, right and wrong. Polarities
serve us in our learning and growth, but as soul we are all.

JOY PAGE

YOU WILL RECALL that the etheric body is the energetic bridge
between the spiritual and the physical levels of vibration, as well as acting as the template for the physical body. The physical level of being
has an apparently dual nature, reflected in the poles of opposites with
which we are all familiar, such as light and dark, hot and cold, female
and male, and so on. The poles of opposites are actually relative features of a single continuum. For example, light and darkness are aspects
of light; hot and cold are aspects of temperature; female and male are
aspects of gender.

THE POLARITY CHANNELS
SUPPORT THE ETHERIC BODY

Similarly, the energies that flow into and out of the etheric body are
aspects of the cycle of subtle energy. These receptive and emissive energies

create an energetic polarity that reflects the dual nature of the physical level. Subtle energetic channels allow for the essential flow of the two energy streams. On each side of the central channel and connected to it, the two channels extend from the base center to meet at the brow center. These two channels, with their links to the central channel, support the whole etheric body. The circulation of energy in the two channels creates a balance between the inflow and outflow of energies throughout the subtle energy system. When these polarities are in balance, our dual identity as spiritual, as well as physical, beings is revealed and maintained.

The energy polarities are often referred to as *masculine* and *feminine,* based on the relative roles of male and female in procreation, but these polarity terms describe qualities of energy flow rather than aspects of gender. For the purposes of understanding soul and heart-centeredness, this book refers to the polarities as the receptive/feminine and emissive/ masculine energy streams respectively. Every person, without exception,

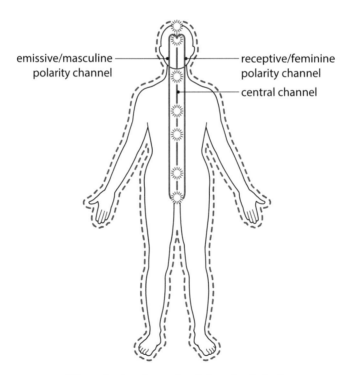

emissive/masculine polarity channel

receptive/feminine polarity channel

central channel

The polarity channels of the etheric body

has both channels and both energies. The emissive, right side of the light body processes energies that are outgoing, as the receptive left side processes energies that are incoming. This is the same for everyone.

There is greater acknowledgment today of the whole breadth of gender that exists between the two poles of the so-called male and female. All persons have within them the two energy streams that are ideally in a state of balance. A woman does not have more receptive energy than a man, and a man does not have more emissive energy than a woman. However, this initial energetic balance may be upset, particularly by cultural or societal norms, such as the predominance of one group over another or one gender over another.

The two energy streams in every individual ensure that they can fully partake in life. They originate at a subtle level as the soul engages with the duality of physical existence. The subtle origin of the energetic rhythm of giving and receiving is about creation itself. Oneness/the Source gives out, or emits, all the beings of creation in an outpouring of energy. The next instant it receives back that outpouring of energy, changed as it has become through the energetic interaction of all life-forms. In this way, Oneness is evolving with each giving and receiving.

The universe is a series of dualities by which movement, change, and evolution occur through the rhythm of balance and imbalance between the pairs of dualities. Our very breathing exemplifies the whole concept of the dualities. We breathe in—we receive—there is a pause; then we breathe out—we give out, we emit—there is another pause before we breathe in again. When we come into the world and take that first breath, we are receptive, we take in the world around us. When we leave the world at the moment of the death of our physical body, we breathe out for the last time. Our last act as a worldly being is to give our breath to the world, and later, our body gives its organic components to the Earth. The act of breathing tells us about the fact of duality, the fact that duality has a rhythm, that life is rhythm, and that living is about receiving and giving. The duality in life is reflected again in the two streams of energy within us. This is how it is.

THE DRAMA OF OUR LUMINOSITY

The seven main energy centers operate in this rhythmic way. They receive and give out energy. When we come to look at the essential function of light in the life of the world and in our own lives we see at once the rhythm of the dualities of which light and dark are both a part.

The rhythm of light and dark, mirrored in our breathing, also reminds us of the journey of the soul. The so-called dark night of the soul is another period in the journey toward the light when the whole being feels immersed in darkness on every level. The drama of life here is the forgetting by the personality of its sacred origins and then the remembrance of who we really are. There are periods of total immersion in life—the receptive, inward-moving time—and then there is the gradual emergence of the soul as it expresses through life, which is the emissive, outward-moving time. Our forgetting and remembering is a drama about our own luminosity.

When we understand and develop relationship with the dualities, we realize that they actually reveal the spiritual vastness of Creation. To see them simply as a series of opposites or antagonistic opposites is a tragic misunderstanding. Our progress toward healing and wholeness is therefore to move forward from past crises to trusting the guidance of soul—the feminine force of enlightenment: reconnection with Oneness.

The flow of energies within and without each one of us is, in reality, one cycle. The next Pilgrimage Action gives you an experience of the dual aspects and the oneness of the energy streams.

Pilgrimage Action 11

Merging the Energy Streams

✦ Go outdoors if possible and find a place where you will not be disturbed. Stand with your arms by your sides. Take three slow, full breaths as you relax your body.

✦ Now raise both hands in front of you, palms up, to the level of your chest. Imagine that there is a line of light that divides your body exactly in half, from your head to your feet. Take a look into each side of your body. Is each side filled with light or is there some darkness in places? Relax. Do not make any judgment about what you sense.

✦ Imagine that you can breathe in the universal energy around you as light. First, you will breathe this light into the left, "feminine," side of your body. Breathe the light into the energy center in your left palm.

✦ Allow the light you have breathed in to spread up your left arm to the shoulder and from there to fill the left side of your body, including your left leg and left foot. Keep breathing gently in this way until you sense that the left side of your body is filled with new light. Maintain your relaxed position.

✦ Still standing, with your arms by your sides, take three slow, full breaths as you relax your body.

✦ Now you will follow the same breathing action with the right, "masculine," side of your body. Raise both hands in front of you, palms up, to the level of your chest. Imagine the same line of light that divides your body exactly in half, from your head to your feet. Take a look into the right side of your body. Is this side filled with light or is there some darkness in places? Relax. Do not make any judgment about what you sense.

✦ Imagine that you can breathe in the universal energy around you as light. Breathe the light into the energy center in your right palm.

✦ Allow the light you have breathed in to spread up your right arm to the shoulder and from there to fill the right side of your body, including your right leg and right foot. Keep breathing gently in this way until you sense that the right side of your body is filled with new light. Maintain your relaxed position.

✦ Still standing, with your arms by your sides, take three slow, full breaths as you relax your body.

✦ Notice how the two energy streams endeavor to balance each other.

✦ Now raise both hands in front of you again, palms up, to the level of your chest. As you stand, imagine that you can breathe in the universal energy around you, as light, into the energy center at the top of your head: the crown center. As this light pours down into your body, allow the light in the two sides of your body to balance and then merge. Keep breathing gently in this way until you sense that your whole body is filled with the one new light.

+ You are part of the cycle of energy that pours into life on Earth from the Source. Enjoy the sensation of being part of this energy cycle as it constantly moves in this way throughout all forms, including the mineral, plant, animal, and human.

+ Finally give thanks for the cycle of energy that pervades you, the Earth, and the universe.

THE OPPRESSION OF THE RECEPTIVE/FEMININE ENERGY STREAM

For emotional and mental health, as well as physical well-being, the energies of the two polarities should be free-flowing and in a state of balance. However, it is easy for them to become blocked or out of balance. Our mental or emotional states, our thoughts or behavior, have an instant effect on this balance. If this goes on for too long so that one energy stream is unused or underdeveloped, the other compensates by dominating the system and all its activities. In this way, it is possible to have too much receptive energy or too much emissive energy.

Historically, a very serious aspect of this state of affairs has been the norm: the blocking and oppression of the receptive energy stream by centuries of patriarchy. We have lived for thousands of years with the effects of the gendering of the energy streams. The heart directs us to repair this by achieving balance between the two energy streams, which have their origin in the base center. In so doing, the heart center confronts worldwide aggression, lack of compassion, and disregard for life itself.

The Inner Circle Teachings emphasize the important relationship between soul and the receptive/feminine. To distance ourselves from the receptive/feminine is to distance ourselves from our true nature and the Source/Oneness. While mental energies are linked to the emissive/ masculine energy stream, soul is accessed by, and represented by, the receptive/feminine energy stream. The full expression of soul depends on the free flow of this stream. Part of our mission as soul beings is to restore the receptive/feminine energy stream at all levels of life. This will be achieved through heart-centeredness, a process that begins with accessing soul guidance in the heart center.

6

SACRED SPACE

Soul and the Heart Center

Dwelling within all beings is the soul self, a little flame in the heart. Those who know their soul will reach the supreme spirit, Brahman (Oneness).

KATHA UPANISHAD

SINCE ANCIENT TIMES, every culture has built its life around what it considers to be a sacred space—a center. It might be a building, a temple, a city, or simply a home; it might be a place outdoors, such as a mountain, a water source, a grove, or a clearing. Some cultures have even made their sacred center a person, such as a monarch, priestess, priest, or shaman. Each represents a point where contact can be made with Oneness/the Source. It is a point where heaven and Earth converge, where human life meets the transcendent life of the spirit. Therefore, the historical function of the sacred center was to provide a means of contact with the sacred so that human life did not become dominated by the demands and desires of individual ego-minds.

We do not need history to tell us that even having created all kinds of sacred space around the world has not ensured that human beings are guided by unconditional love and the wisdom of the soul. We need to be heart centered when we enter a space dedicated to the sacred, but what goes on in the space may not put us in touch with our heart. When this is the case, no religion or spiritual teaching will change the dominance of the ego-mind. Instead, religions and teachings become used for power and material gain. The missing link is the heart. This is why the wisdom teachings of heart-centeredness are always revolutionary at whatever time and wherever they appear. The teachings of perennial wisdom, as taught in the Inner Circle Teachings, are relevant to all times and all places.

We are at a crucial point in human and planetary evolution because we have reached a tipping point where we are close to choosing the extinction of all life on our planet. The Inner Circle Teachings counsel that the way out of the situation can only be via a return to heart-centeredness and the guidance of the soul. Our planet was created for the soul to express the Source within physicality. The human being is key to this soul expression. We are here to *be* God, to be Oneness.

How to do this has been presented to us for millennia, though the ego-mind has convinced us otherwise. However, the mind has run out of time to find ego-based solutions to our massive global problems. Meanwhile the call of the heart can still be heard, assuring us that we can trust the guidance of soul to reveal the way forward to peace and harmony for all people. Perhaps we are now ready to hear the call and to listen. Entering the heart center to access this guidance is simple—it has to be! Access and communication is the first step. If we want to make a difference, regular practice must follow. Here is the core activity of the Inner Circle Teachings.

✳ Pilgrimage Action 12
Accessing the Heart Center

Make sure you are fully conversant with the previous exercises relating to breathing, relaxation, and the subtle energy centers.

+ Find a comfortable position in which you can use your breathing to relax your body. Once relaxed, you are going to breathe into your heart center. Recall that this center is in the center of your chest. You might like to put your hand over this spot to remind you of its position and to focus your attention. This is where you can gain access to soul guidance.

✦ Close your eyes (this sends a signal to your mind that you are present to yourself and thus detaching from external stimulation). Allow your mind to rest on your breath.

✦ Now breathe slowly and gently into your heart center until you feel settled there. Acknowledge your soul—your soul has been waiting for this moment. Keep breathing until you feel, or sense, your soul's presence. This may feel like a tingling in the hands or a gentle pressure in some part of your body.

✦ Enjoy the feeling of simply being in soul presence. Enjoy the calm and silence of soul presence.

✦ Once you are aware of soul presence you can begin communication with your soul.

You can check whether you are in touch with soul by asking a simple question and waiting for an answer. Once you become confident that you can communicate with your soul you will find that its guidance will usually surprise you. It will not use flowery or contrived language, nor will it announce that it is from another star or galaxy. Remember, your ego-mind will try to interrupt and give its own message. You will soon learn to recognize your mind by its language—it can only supply what is already in its database. When accessing the soul, there is nothing to learn at the level of ego-mind.

Your soul is your spiritual reality. As you work with this book you will find that the separation gap between your ego-mind and your soul consciousness begins to close. Ultimately, there will be moments when you will become aware of a single consciousness. This is what you will be working toward. Your soul can explain to you in simple language what your purpose in life is, where you came from, and where you will return to. If your communication ever seems complicated or long-winded, you can be sure that your ego-mind has interfered and is trying to take over and reverse your progress in your alignment with your real identity and your link with Oneness/the Source.

CALLING ON THE DIVINE FEMININE

You can live your life by what others are telling you—by what you think society, your family, and your friends expect of you. You may think that you are the one making all the decisions, but you are just reacting to your environment, basing your life on how your mind interprets what is happening around you. You are continually reinforcing your ego and your mind's reactions, leaving you disempowered as a true creator.

Feminine wisdom offers a different way of being and living. This is to call upon the divine feminine by accessing your heart center and by connecting with beauty, compassion, and oneness in your life. The divine feminine is never concerned with separation. The mind functions by separating and labeling what it has separated. This means that you cannot connect with the divine feminine through your mind alone. The divine feminine is the acknowledgment of your divine nature through your heart. When you live according to your heart's guidance, you make decisions and choices based on this inner guidance, acting from a place of unconditional love rather than separation and fear. By acknowledging and including the divine feminine, soul becomes your guide, illuminating a way to create a more fulfilling life. You become a more loving, caring person who has respect for yourself and all life-forms around you.

STAGES OF HEART-CENTEREDNESS

Becoming heart centered happens in four basic stages, rather like the levels of initiation in the ancient mystery schools. At first, we begin with our normal everyday level of consciousness, living with our inner perceptions unused or closed. Then we catch glimpses or flashes of awareness as our consciousness opens up through seeking answers. We have unconsciously begun to answer the call of the soul. From such small awakenings we begin to understand that the heart is indeed an organ of perception. We sense that the perception that we are all one is true. Finally, we experience sacred unity—Oneness. We know that sacred unity is the actual reality of life. As we become aware that We Are All One, this awareness (called *gnosis* by the Greeks) is deepened with each experience of Oneness. Awareness becomes knowing. We do not believe, we *know,* and faith appears as sister to this new wisdom. Our faith is based on our experience of knowing, not on systems of belief. Becoming heart centered leads to an understanding and experiencing of the mysteries of life.

Pilgrimage Action 13
Being with Soul Presence

As a natural progression from the previous Pilgrimage Action, this next core activity enables you to sense and then immerse yourself in soul presence. With practice, sensing and being with soul presence will gradually become a familiar companionship.

+ Use your breathing to relax your body. Make sure that you are in a comfortable position where you can remain alert and aware.
+ Put your attention in your heart center. Again, you might like to put your hand over this center. This is where you can gain access to soul presence.
+ Close your eyes (this sends a signal to your mind that you are present to yourself and thus detaching from external stimulation). Allow your mind to rest on your breath.
+ Now breathe slowly and gently into your heart center until you feel settled there. Acknowledge your soul—your soul is waiting for you. Keep breathing until you feel or sense your soul's presence.
+ Your intention is to simply be in soul presence—breathing gently and normally, with your eyes closed. Thoughts may flit in and out of consciousness. Simply allow them to pass through your mind as you calmly remain in soul presence.

✦ Being with soul like this may last from a few moments to much longer.

✦ When you feel ready, let your consciousness return to the place where you are sitting. Become aware of your physical body and surroundings. Ground yourself by rubbing your hands together (heart center) and rubbing your thighs (base center), feeling your feet on the ground. This strengthens the link between the heart center and the base center and reinforces your identity as a spiritual being in a physical body.

Allow yourself a time slot in your day to be with your soul. Any time of day and any place is fine. You can begin your day, before you get out of bed, by accessing your heart center. Perhaps you need some tips on how to deal with what is to come today. Perhaps you just need to go to that place to gently remind yourself about who you are. This will illuminate your approach to the day. Your heart center is your home. From here on you can picture your day as moving out from your home to explore life and the world. Then you return home and review your discoveries. You can finish your day in the same way that you began it. Practice while lying down may well induce total rest or sound sleep.

LOVE BRINGS CHANGES
IN THE ENERGY CENTERS

With the practice of heart-centeredness, the force of unconditional love on the energy centers augments normal, everyday energetic processing with soul wisdom. The effect on the energy centers is twofold. With our minds in control, we have developed illusions about what it means to be human and about life itself. With heart-centeredness, the illusions that we may have about any of the life issues in a particular center begin to be dispelled. This may bring surprises, but they will be positive and constructive. At the same time, each center presents the challenge to move on from the person that you used to be to the new you—a greater, more vital, and more capable version of yourself, your authentic self.

The promise of heart-centeredness is that with soul guidance you will be able to achieve this and more.

The return of unconditional love within the subtle energy system brings new revelations, new possibilities, new courses of action, and provokes new ways of thinking. Mind will be alert to these changes. In the next seven chapters, we will discover how heart-centeredness releases soul energies to profoundly affect the seven main energy centers. Life issues dealt with by each center now take on a new, expanded dimension. The energies encourage us to achievements that we may not have thought we were capable of. They can light up life so that it becomes an adventure.

PART 2

The Seven Energy Centers
Our Human Rainbow

7

LOVE IS RED

The Base Center

The soul is not in the body, the body is in the soul. It is steeped in the soul like a net in the sea.

GIORDANO BRUNO

THE BASE CENTER reminds us that as we leave our spiritual home, the Earth becomes our new home. This is why Earth, and looking after it, is so important. Incarnation marks the separating out from the Source. The impact of this separation, and all the separations that follow it, are registered in the base center. Consciousness now becomes focused on the physical body and its survival.

THE ILLUSIONS AFFECTING THE BASE CENTER

As we have already discovered, over time the mind has taken control of our response to physicality. This has created the unfortunate outcomes of self-centeredness. A function of the base center is to process physical life and our reactions to it. On our pilgrimage to heart-centeredness this is where we encounter our first illusions. These illusions influence life, the body, our senses, and our attitude toward sex, sensuality, the natural world, and planet Earth.

When the heart–base connection is weakened through such illusions, our connection to our bodies and the natural world is weakened. But when we begin to practice the Pilgrimage Actions, the initiatory energies of heart-centeredness prepare the body to receive the higher vibrations of the Light by awakening the ego-personality to its true nature, and to the experience of Oneness. Energetically, reconnections are made in the base center where the initiatory process begins.

The Body

We think the body is who we are. We are conscious of our body and we want it to be our friend. We are conscious of the bodies of others, conscious of how others view their own bodies and how they view our body. It seems important to have a body that is acceptable to other people and to ourselves. This acceptability is reinforced by media images so that we may strive to adapt our body to fit these images. Our need for acceptance influences how we choose to appear, what we choose to wear, where we choose to live, how we choose to live, what we choose to eat, and how we choose to behave.

The base center links us to planet Earth. Its link with the energy centers of the feet reminds us that as spiritual beings in a physical world, our head may be in the clouds, but it is just as essential for us to be connected to both Earth and heaven. We do this by being grounded. Inner Circle Teachings advise us to celebrate physicality and to find ways of staying grounded—being involved in physical intimacy; having the responsibilities of family life; expressing one's sexuality; eating, drinking, merrymaking, and joking. All these are as essential to our journey experience as entering the silence or the contemplation of beauty, for these are the foundations of safe and healthy transformation.

The Challenge of Aging

We accept the natural rhythms in Nature—birth, growth, decline, death—but do we accept that we too have this natural growth cycle? As we get older, we encounter changes in the body due to its natural process of aging. How will these changes affect our relationship with our body? Will others see us in a different way as we age? The natural aging processes of the body remind us that one day we will die so we had better put off that day by staying young. We may strive to keep a youthful body image and take steps to keep the body as fit as possible. We may adapt our behavior to show ourselves and others that we are not "old," we are not really aging. But when we look in the mirror we see that we cannot escape these natural processes. We are reminded that aging is part of our natural cycle. The day will come when we realize that there are activities that we can no longer perform with ease. Our relationship with physical life and the planet is changing. It is a fact of natural law. This will happen no matter how many cosmetic operations we may have. Denial of these changes simply reinforces the illusion.

Relationship

We are social beings in societies that are founded on relationships. Illusion means that we lose sight of each other as souls on a sacred journey. From a cynical viewpoint, relationships have to have a purpose. Heart-centeredness reminds us that the soul has come to the body and to physical life for the spiritual purpose of evolution. We are evolving. We are becoming. With illusion, we are using our relationship with everything and everyone to decide what we are becoming.

Pain and Suffering

The base center demands that we look after the body. As we awaken to this challenge we can begin to address the imbalance within our subtle energetic anatomy upon which the physical body is founded. This disharmony is frequently reflected in the body as disease and illness. Disharmony can be addressed by first examining our thoughts and behaviors, and then by carefully looking at the world around us that we have helped create.

In spite of the inevitability of the aging process, the body does its best to keep us fit and healthy. It can only do this if we cooperate with its signals—about what to eat, where to live, how to live, the right environment, the right activities, for example. Mind will try to suppress body knowledge. The physical body is also affected by our thoughts and emotions, whether they are positive or negative. Our energy centers process all life issues and may send their own signals to us about how to remedy a state or situation that is affecting our well-being or security. If we fail to heed their signals, the energetic message is passed to the body as the last resort. The body then has the task of alerting us and it will do this in the most appropriate way. Ultimately this can manifest as illness or disease. Illness and disease change our view of our body and life. Pain and suffering can completely dominate how we feel and what we do. It may seem that our body is not our friend after all. No matter how hard we have tried, our body has let us down.

These feelings are natural, but they are also the outcome of experiencing that the body is all that we are. Unconditional love has the power to help us realize that we are more than our body—we are spiritual beings *with* a body. The body is sacred and we should treat it as such. Heart-centeredness will help us have compassion for the body that has tried to serve us, as well as compassion for our own pain or suffering. We will learn that we are more than any pain or suffering and more than any physical condition.

Gender

Most of us come into the world with two identifiable parents, a mother and a father. This naturally supports our early illusions about gender. "My mother is the female and my father is the male." Then as we grow up we discover that these genders simply represent two polarities and that there are many variations of gender between the polarities. Our cultural norm may insist that there are only the two polarities of gender and, according to our gender, only two ways of behaving. This is illusion. The truth shows us a different picture.

We know that temperature is not just about hot and cold, and that there are endless variations in temperature in between the two polarities. We have no choice but to accept this seeming reality of physicality. Unconditional love reveals that the world is far more complex than we first thought, than our family first thought, than those around us first thought, than our society first thought, than our country first thought. It reveals that within each pair of dualities, there are endless combinations, ranging from one duality to the other. These realities hold as much for gender and sexuality issues as they do for our unconscious acceptance of everyday realities like temperature. This is how it is—whether we like it or not. The base center holds on to this truth.

In the state of harmony we call peace, difference is accepted and even celebrated rather than argued about or fought over. Peace comes from a balance between all the dualities, including those of giving and receiving, of sending out and allowing in, at all levels. Heart-centeredness encourages us to look at our thoughts and behaviors around both poles of duality and everything that lies between those poles.

Nature

Our great illusion about the natural world stems from the fact that we can cut it up, dissect it, analyze it, manipulate it, exploit it, change it, own it, even create it, and so dominate it. This illusion also extends to everything about the planet itself that sustains us—the Earth with its soil and water resources, the air we breathe, the food we eat. We think that we know how the natural world and the planet operate so we are obviously in a position to use them for our own ends. The mind message is one of control and domination.

Soul presence removes the illusion of separation and restores our place in Nature. If you allow it, any facet of Nature can reach out, like soul, to embrace you and remove the illusion of separation.

PAYING ATTENTION AND MEDITATION

Heart-centeredness in the base center transforms the processing of our interaction with the natural world into the key practice of paying attention. The mystery of a rock or tree, a plant, an animal, or a person, is about being aware of the clue or wisdom that they offer. It will be something that seems relevant to your own life journey. The clues and the wisdom are concealed in every being that you encounter, even the sounds, scents, and every touch. The clues concealed in creation are calling forth your own mystery, the real person that you are. The more that you pay attention, the more you allow creation to unfold its mystery.

From time to time, we need to send the mind into "exile" during the day, just as our waking consciousness goes into exile during sleep and we are free to dream. A way to ensure this exile of the mind is through the method of paying attention known as meditation. Meditation is the natural state when we are not trying to do anything. Meditation is to be here now, in this moment. Doing nothing is to be effortless, the state children are in when they play. Play is effortless to them, for they are in a state of meditation. Watch your breath. You are paying attention to your breathing. It arises and subsides. This teaches us that everything arises and subsides. In other words, everything is impermanent. Everything has this cycle. In the next activity you can move effortlessly from paying attention to meditation.

 **Pilgrimage Action 14**

A Meditation in Nature

+ Go out into natural surroundings and find a comfortable place to sit. Take a few slow, deep breaths as you contemplate the scenery around you. Just take in the wonder of what is around you and what you sense beneath your feet.

+ Allow your mind to settle in the heart center. Offer a prayer or blessing to all that is around and beneath you. Now you can ask for a wisdom teaching, for guidance, or for whatever is appropriate for you at this time.

+ Do not anticipate anything or direct your thoughts. Allow thoughts that arise to simply pass through your mind without grasping at them.

+ If you find yourself following their trend, return to your heart place. Sit in the silence or the sounds around you.

✦ When you feel ready, let your consciousness return to the place where you are sitting. Become aware of your physical body and surroundings. Ground yourself by rubbing your hands together (heart center) and rubbing your thighs (base center), feeling your feet on the ground. This strengthens the link between the heart center and the base center and reinforces your identity as a spiritual being in a physical body.

In this form of meditation you are *experiencing* your environment rather than observing it. You are in the moment. You are paying attention to the mystery. This stepping back from, and letting go of, the need to achieve something allows us to draw closer to the mystery and allows it to reveal itself in its own way.

One of the simplest ways to begin to open your heart center is to link with the natural world in every way you can. It may seem strange at first, but if you embrace it, you will soon enjoy linking with the day itself, sunlight and moonlight, the weather as sky, clouds, wind, and rain. You can link with plants and animals, no matter how small or seemingly insignificant. Begin by acknowledging them, thanking them, talking to them, and showing that you are open to hearing them and listening to them. Notice how the relationship builds and how easy it is for love to flow between you and the beings of Nature. It is easier to do this with them than it is with humans. Nature can only give you unconditional love. With Nature you not only open your heart but learn about love.

UNCONDITIONAL LOVE SHATTERS ILLUSIONS

If illusions are shattered or dispelled, there are consequences in the form of challenges that we would rather not face. Unconditional love will shatter our illusions with the startling revelation that We Are All One. When this is realized, we first have to change our attitudes with regard to those around us, to all other human beings, to the whole natural world and all its functions, and to the planet and all its functions. With changes of attitude come big changes in behavior. The revelation that We Are All One is in opposition to the mind's insistence that our behavior is the rightful outcome of our separation from each other and from everything else in the world—and this is based on what appears to be evidence, isn't it?

The challenge is twofold. First we recognize the illusion for what it is. Secondly, we have to be willing to let go of it. Unconditional love meets the challenge. This is heart-centeredness. Heart-centeredness does not just shatter our illusions. With soul guidance we can move forward from the illusions we once held to address the challenges raised by the upgraded base center. Heart-centeredness can train the mind to serve soul guidance. Human endeavor, in whatever field, can be used to attain equality between all human beings, rather than to further the self-centered aims of some. Science, for example, can be used to encourage our companionship with, and our respect for, the natural world.

The wisdom of the heart teaches that we are *all* travelers on planet Earth, without exception, and that we have to journey together. The base center records the illusion of what is and is constantly struggling with the truth of what should be.

The impact of unconditional love on each center creates opportunities for psychological unity and personal transformation. Each opportunity says: Here you are presented with the chance and the choice for change. What will you do? In the base center the opportunity is to turn the everyday into the sacred, to integrate the feminine and masculine energy streams within yourself, and to change who you appear to be to who you really are. The base center is our sacred umbilical link to Mother Earth.

8

LOVE IS ORANGE

The Sacral Center

Every child comes into the world with a message.
RABINDRANATH TAGORE

THE SACRAL CENTER supports the creative expression of soul and processes our life issues around creativity, sexuality, and expressions of joy. This center is also the place of our true self that came into being as a playful, creative, and joyful child of love—the "inner child."

THE INNER CHILD

The inner child represents the joining of the soul with the life of physicality. The golden inner child preserves all the soul qualities that shine through the children who are loved for who and what they are. Heart-centeredness challenges any illusions we may have about sacral center issues and awakens us to acknowledge and renew our relationship with our own inner child again. Heart's counsel is to retrieve the wisdom of our inner child.

Being childlike is an inner response to our undamaged and love-nurtured self. Being childlike, being spontaneous, is essential to creativity and opens the channel for having the actual experience of joy as an energy generated in the sacral center. We are able to feel the wonder of creation, the wonder of the natural world, the wonder of other people, and the magic of life experience. This is soul's promise to the infant human.

Much has been written about how important elements of the personality are formed in the early years of childhood, especially the effects of early experience on creativity and the ability to be authentic, to be *real*. From many years of research into childhood relationships, the pediatrician and psychoanalyst D. W. Winnicott (1896–1971) considered that one of the key elements of personality that could be lost in childhood was the capacity to feel genuinely alive. He saw this as essential to the maintenance of a true self. The true self, he declared, is fostered by the practice of childhood play—having feelings that are spontaneous and unforced.

The experience of aliveness is what allows people to be genuinely close to others and to be creative. But when the infant is not given unconditional love in its early life, it will tend to develop a defense in the form of a mask of behavior that allows it to comply with the expectations of others. This illusory aspect of the developing personality causes it to suffer from a sense of emptiness, of being dead or false. What does it have to do to be loved?

Our inner child may seem distant from our everyday consciousness, someone in our past whom we may or may not remember well. What our body and emotions remember, however, is how we were treated as a child. A simple way to discover this is to notice what presses our emotional buttons—what events or situations invoke one or more negative emotions, such as fear, anger, resentment, sadness, and despair. None of these emotions or feelings emerge from a place of love, caring, compassion, or kindness—quite the opposite. Our reactions are telling us that our inner child needs healing.

THE CREATIVE ASPECT OF THE SACRAL CENTER

The heart teaches that with soul guidance we can become cocreators with the Source/Oneness. We see that all forms of creativity are prime ways of expressing the sacred. The initiatory energy of the soul awakens our inner child, which in turn activates our own creative "womb." A characteristic of all children is that they play, in all situations. If we can't play—can't be creative, can't use our imagination, can't have fun, can't enjoy life without some technological help, have no sense of wonder—something needs healing in the sacral center. When this is the case, it usually concerns the inner child.

Despite hearing the voice of the heart, we tend to listen to the voice of the conditioned mind with its illusory messages about what can and what cannot be achieved. We may have received such messages from childhood onward. When we seek to express our own creativity or our spontaneity there is often an inner conflict between the two voices and about which one we should listen to.

Issues around outside authority tend to arise because being creative is being Godlike. When what stops us from being creative is an actual outer authority, reference to the heart center and soul guidance can help find ways around the situation. When the voice comes from an inner authority, such as the mind's voice of our poor self-image, saying that we cannot be Godlike, we may feel even more intimidated. Here, reference to the heart center and soul guidance will help to dispel the illusion that we cannot express our creative self.

Creative Imagination

"Every natural effect has a spiritual cause," wrote the eighteenth-century mystic, poet, and artist William Blake. He considered that all religions were one and that the perennial philosophy, wisdom itself, appeared in modern times as the "religion of the creative imagination"—a natural effect of a spiritual cause. The impulse of the creative imagination stems from, encourages, and provides for the expression of the soul. It embodies a creativity that generates beauty and is an expression of joy. The religion of the imagination, when seen as a contemporary interpretation of the perennial philosophy, is a spirituality stripped of rules and regulations and given back to the heart.

When a creative work is made through the promptings of the soul it will contain a life force that can be felt as an emanation from the work. The life force enables the created work to continue to speak to whoever comes into contact with it. However, when the subject matter simply has the appearance of something sacred it has no spiritual power to offer. We know this intuitively if we are alert. We cannot be fooled. But our ego may want us to be fooled when, for example, it is fashionable to like something that has no spiritual power but is stimulating in some other way.

Blake made no distinction between all forms of creative imagination and prophecy, nor between sacred art and religion. Blake's meaning when he described his poems as "prophecies" is derived from the Hebrew word for prophet, *navi,* signifying a bringing forth out of oneself—and the place from which the essence of oneself emanates is the heart. The Inner Circle Teachings indicate that Blake's religion of the imagination is indeed the way of the heart, giving us clues and guidance about how to identify this perennial form of wisdom spirituality. It will be characterized by the poetic and the imaginative and embody heart-centeredness.

Blake believed and affirmed that the ability to contact higher levels of consciousness is not given to a select few but is innate in all of us, though most people are not aware of it. The true prophet is one who summons us to become aware of who we really are, to awaken, and to listen to the voice of soul. Like all such awakeners, Blake spoke from the soul to the heart in all of us.

A creator in our own times, the composer John Tavener (1944–2013), admired the Greeks for their intuitive knowing that spirituality has to embody a wisdom of the heart that is beyond the understanding of the mind. Tavener felt that for a work to truly communicate with others, there had to be a process whereby the nourishment of spiritual practice was taken up by the total being of the composer, assimilated, and turned into life force. The created work could then be given out to the world as a transformative energy—the joy of sound and the joy of spirituality. In all creativity, where the artist is able to communicate with an audience there is this joyful exchange of life force as an expression of the sacred.

Thought and Creativity

In the creative process we are challenged to look at how we think, who we send our thoughts to, and the way we think about life, other people, and the world. For all these thoughts are energies that find their way to their destination where they have an energetic effect. The law of energy is that any thought will attract thoughts like itself, creating a thought cloud. This then becomes a much more powerful energy than the original. Thus thoughts may cause very positive or very negative effects. Few are aware that the energies of thought become matter in the form of things. Yet whatever we see around us that has been made has first been a thought or a collection of thoughts, and this applies as much to situations as to things. Anyone who has ever created anything will testify to this.

The call of the soul is so urgent because we are going to have to deal with what has been created in our world through all the negative thinking, worry, and anxiety, especially the unkindness and destructiveness, the constant portrayal of evil, anger, and despair presented in the media. Mind has singularly failed to solve the problem of the devastating effects of negative thinking on creativity and the provision of facilities for creativity. Heart-centeredness in the sacral center tells us that only the guidance of soul is capable of turning the tide. It is time we gave unconditional love a chance.

Pilgrimage Action 15
Expressing the Joy of Life—
Opening to Universal Energies

When we stand with our arms above our head, it is a natural expression of joy. Do you recall dancing like this? Have you witnessed the spectators waving their arms in the air at a sporting event or pop concert? This joy creates positive feelings and attracts positive energies for you and all around you. The next activity shows how to harness this natural expression of joy.

+ Stand on the ground in a relaxed posture with your feet a shoulder-width apart. Take six slow, full breaths. Raise your head and breathe normally as you look up at the sky and beyond.

+ Put your attention in the soles of your feet. Be aware of your contact with the Earth.

+ Raise your arms above your head and stretch them out, with your palms upward. You are reaching up to the heavens, the spiritual realm.

+ The sun gives life to our planet. It can represent the life-giving light from where we came. Visualize that you can breathe the energies of the sun into your palm centers. Even if the sun is not visible, you can still breathe in its energies.

+ Enjoy the sensation of these energies entering and then circulating throughout your body. As you exhale, give out the energies to the world.

+ Visualize that you can breathe in the energies of the sky. Enjoy the sensation of these energies entering and then circulating throughout your body. As you exhale, give out the energies to the world.

+ Allow your imagination to extend further. Visualize that you can breathe in the benevolent energies of the cosmos. Enjoy the sensation of these energies entering and then circulating throughout your body, your subtle anatomy, and your energy field (aura). As you exhale, you are giving out the energies to All That Is.

+ You may feel the need to give out the energies as sound—shout, laugh, sigh—or other body movements. Let it happen! Finally, slowly lower your arms and relax. How good does that feel?

Sacred Sex

Joy comes from the creative process, particularly when it happens in conjunction with the energies of the heart center as unconditional love.

The joy in creativity is the outcome of the oneness that occurs between the creator and the created. Distance exists where we as creator feel separate from what we have created. This becomes most serious when it concerns a child as the created being.

Our sexual activity is processed in the sacral center as creativity. With the practice of heart-centeredness, the energies of unconditional love challenge us to look again at our sexual activity and sexual experience. Sex can be a centering prayer and a meditation on Oneness when we make ourselves totally present to the body, mind, and soul of another. Candles, incense, perfume, music, flowers, wine, and song are used in romance, sex, and love, as well as in religious ritual and ceremony. The true sexual experience, like the mystical experience, is a passionate, transcendent activity. But before we can think of sex as an act of deep communion with Oneness and our oneness with another, it has to be reclaimed from the illusions created by the prejudices and phobias of many religions, cultures, and traditions. When sex is a creative act, like all creative acts, it is sacred. A total celebration of the sacrament of sex requires the healing of distorted notions about the body, its functions, and needs. We may also need to heal the wounds that are present in our own sexual past.

THE "OTHER"

Just as the base center deals with the survival of the individual in terms of the body, the sacral center deals with the next phase of the development of the personality: awareness of the "other." As we grow and develop we become aware that there are other people out there—such as parents, guardians, and caregivers—and, eventually, that there is a world of others outside of us.

The energies of unconditional love give us a fresh perspective about our body and the natural world. This perspective now extends into, and brings changes to, our concept of the other. We have lived with the illusion that all others were separate from us. Sometimes this has been convenient—we do not have to be responsible for others. Then, when others upset the balance of our lives, we are relieved that they are separate from us. Heart-centeredness challenges these self-centered thoughts and feelings with the painful truth that our concept of the other is an illusion.

In the base center there is an acknowledgment and understanding of all dualities being united in Oneness. Unconditional love makes this an actual experience. The ancient mystery schools called this actuality "sacred marriage." In the sacral center, heart-centeredness moves us further to an understanding and experience that *me* and the *other* are actually one.

INTEGRATION

In the process of shattering another illusion about our concept of self, the energies of unconditional love challenge us to unite the disparate parts of our self. These are parts that we may not have known very well, parts that we have denied, or parts that we may not have realized even existed. These are the lost parts of ourselves that have become distant from our true self. Soul teaches that we can integrate those parts of ourselves that had once appeared distant, split off, even when this had seemed a distant dream. This releases healing and creativity. Joy is released as we make the discovery of the real "us." This is further enhanced by the experience of conscious connection with the soul and the sacral center.

SOUL CAN CLOSE ALL DISTANCES

As soul dispels our illusions about what distance and separation really are, we see the need for healing the effects of our illusions. Heart-centeredness shows us our own distancing and, where necessary, the need to guide our inner child back home.

The sacral center reminds us that healing is a creative act that is possible because We Are All One. It has to be accepted as a normal and essential part of life *because* We Are All One. Through this link with the sacred, we know that help will be given. When we send out healing thoughts and vibrations to someone, we can sense it as the transmission of subtle energy. The loving thought sent out to another, or to a situation or place, is an energy pattern that when directed with intention will have a positive effect.

Heart-centeredness in the sacral center proves that healing energy travels outside of the space/time continuum. Thus we have the opportunity to send help to someone at a distance, even to be of anonymous service and help to someone we may never meet. This deep meaning of distant healing is about how the creative energies of unconditional love can dispel the illusion of separation between ourselves and others, and can heal the wounds of disconnection. How we think and feel about this will be processed in the next energy center.

9

LOVE IS GOLDEN YELLOW

The Solar Center

Self is the only prison that can ever bind the soul.

HENRY VAN DYKE

THE SOLAR CENTER is the largest of the seven energy centers and is the vibrant powerhouse of mind and emotion. Just as planet Earth revolves around the sun, so does human life revolve around the activities of the solar center. This center is the scene of the great battle that has been going on for thousands of years—the battle between fear and love, between mind and heart/soul, between the solar center and the heart center.

Mind has told us that fear-based action, in the form of strength and might, will protect us and give us security. Yet, contrary to the expectations of mind's message, history tells us that fear does not win the battle. Fear-based action does not protect us in the long run, and most of all, it does not bring us love, comfort, and security. We merely survive.

For some the journey toward heart-centeredness ends here. The ego-personality is still in the grip of illusions and a way of being and a lifestyle that reinforces these illusions. With no awareness of a sacred identity, the rainbow remains incomplete.

Heart-centeredness rises to the challenge of the solar center to expose mind's fear-based illusions and to explain how our illusions have come about.

THE FUNCTION OF FEAR

The solar center processes life issues around the personality, our sense of identity, and who we think we are. As our personality has developed, who we think we are is a reflection of our self-confidence, our sense of personal power, how we think and react, and what we fear. Mind is directly involved in solar center processing, and its central influence on the whole subtle energy system is the evolutionary outcome of the function of fear.

For our very distant ancestors, fear was necessary for survival. If they did not have fears about unknown landscapes, climatic features, and food supply, if they did not fear wild animals or the hostile attacks of other human beings, they would not have survived. A glance at the natural world shows how the function of fear is the key factor in survival. The part of the human to oversee the operation of fear, in terms of survival, was mind. Fear is processed in the solar center so that this center became the place of mind, just as the heart center is the place of soul and unconditional love.

Over time as life became less dangerous, the natural pressure to survive was extended to other matters. The nurturing and caring of the mother and other relatives, the food-finding, defense, and support of the father and others were also seen as crucial to survival. People had *things* that they needed; people had things that they had enjoyed creating or simply enjoyed having. Owning things became part of survival, as needs began to include the wants and desires of the personality. Any attempt to deprive a person of any of the things now considered necessary for survival is a threat that triggers the initial function of fear.

The love-based qualities that were originally needed for survival were love, caring, and comfort. During human evolution it seemed that these qualities did not keep people safe and did not ensure survival. Furthermore, it seemed that what was wanted and desired could not be had by being loving and caring. Unconditional love asks us to share when mind tells us that clearly there is only so much of anything. Mind tells us that we cannot trust the heart to get us what we want and desire. If we are to survive we must grab what we can, or even grab as much as we can—symptoms of the illusion that there is never enough.

MIND CREATES ILLUSIONS
IN ALL OUR ENERGY CENTERS

Over time, mind in the solar center becomes the guide for human life. Every mind is conditioned from birth to struggle to get what is necessary for personal survival. Thus the mind that is guiding the personality is conditioned—it does not have the clear perception of the heart but is motivated by its self-centered interpretation of life. In this way, we have evolved with illusions in every energy center because mind has come to be the dominant influence in the processes of every center.

Mind's dominance, via the solar center, creates the tendency for us to have illusions about love. Mind's message is that love is actually a survival need. We want what we think is love, we want to be validated by others. If we have illusions about love, we will mistake the behavior of others as signals of approval. We may think that our sexuality and sexual activity can be used to gain love or what we want, or both. We may think that we can get love, approval, or what we want by giving *things* or services to certain others. Relationships may be cultivated in order to gain approval or get what we want. Behavior such as unthinking agreement and flattery may stem from the same needs.

These ways of thinking, feeling, and behaving are fear-based. The mind message is that if we do not think, speak, and act so as to gain the approval of others, we will not get what we want, we will not be validated, and we will not be loved. The subconscious message is "you will not survive."

To fulfill its wants and desires around survival, the personality may convince itself that it can give love to another or is *in love*. Such feelings are a delusion when this form of self-centered love has expectations. The personality will be disappointed, even angry, if its expectations are not realized. The safety valve of suffering tells us that an action and, perhaps, even thoughts and words were motivated by the mind's urging to achieve our wants and desires. Unconditional love cannot cause suffering because it has no expectations.

VITALITY ENERGY

The solar center is the keeper of our personal power. It is the center that is able to draw in vitality energy from the cosmos, especially the sun. Fear makes us believe that we can just as easily lose vitality energy if we squander it in heart-centered activities, such as caring for others. As we shall see in the next chapter, this is another of mind's illusions based on the fear that there might not be enough cosmic energy to go around! The heart has the antidote to this illusion.

However, if you ever feel low in vitality or you want to give yourself an energy boost, the following activity will raise your vitality levels.

Pilgrimage Action 16
Absorbing and Conserving Vitality

+ Stand or sit comfortably with your feet flat on the ground. Use your breathing to relax your body, and visualize your feet making good contact with the ground.

+ Bring your mind to your solar center. You are going to breathe the vitality energy of the sun into your solar center as golden-yellow light. This is the vibratory color of the balanced solar center. As you breathe in the light, slowly and gently, visualize it filling your solar center and then the whole of your abdomen.

+ Continue to breathe in the golden-yellow light and now allow it to flow into the rest of your body. Take your time to allow this.

+ Enjoy the feeling of the sun's vitality energy filling your body. When you feel ready, continue with your day.

Stressful situations and even tending to the needs of others can become a drain on your vitality energy.

+ To ensure that this does not happen, or to make sure that your new energy boost does not ebb away, visualize that you can place a golden disc of light over your solar center.
+ Whenever you feel the need, remind yourself to put your solar disc in place.

REMOVING MENTAL PARALYSIS FROM THE SOLAR CENTER

Fear of the future or fear of moving from one's position are symptoms of mental paralysis. In the solar center, heart-centeredness reveals that if we have suffered from any form of mental paralysis, we have been disconnected from the sacred. We are asked to look at where we have been paralyzed in any area of life. We may have blocked our progress, or sabotaged the emergence and use of our talents, and thereby allowed stagnation and inertia to dictate our lifestyle. This could have been our fear reaction to someone else's influence.

Heart-centeredness has the power to heal the effects of being disconnected from our true selves, to dissolve illusory barriers, and to help us venture beyond any negative mind messages. We have the opportunity to release what has seized up, to unblock a situation, and to break free from the grip of pessimistic feelings.

Forgiveness

The energies of unconditional love impress the solar center to release what is stuck, stagnant, not moving, and devoid of life force. At a deep level, this is what forgiveness is all about. It is as much about the negative effects of blocked energies as regret, remorse, sorrow, and bitterness. When people forgive they release each other, for both are stuck at a point in time. The same goes for any situation that needs healing in this way. When we have regrets about the past we take ourselves back to that time and place, and we stop ourselves from flowing forward in life. We can keep ourselves and others trapped in that same place and time through the inability to forgive or to seek forgiveness. We may need to forgive another, or others, or even ourselves. This must be done if life is to move on and not become stagnant.

When that child of fear and hate—vengeance—is sought, anger or bitterness is seething and forgiveness is difficult. But revenge and anger are destructive and simply enchain each person involved. Revenge can *never* heal anything, nor bring justice. Only forgiveness can do this. Forgiveness is an act of unconditional love. It comes from heart-centeredness and heart emanations always heal. So forgiveness is a necessary energetic process that keeps the cycle of energies turning—that is, life affirming. Vengeance is the way of death and is life annulling.

The loving guidance of soul is that thinking of the past in a negative way, such as past regrets, takes us out of the present—our existential reality—and backward into a place that is now purely an illusory creation of the mind. Being out of the present prevents our moving forward. By maintaining our awareness in the heart-centered present we will progress naturally without having to think about it.

The key to all healthy relationships is forgiveness, nonjudgment, and compassion. If we do not understand this, we will accumulate energetic debts to others that will become more and more difficult to repay. This is how the soul operates with us. To be aligned with soul we will have to be the same. We need to be able to recognize when we are out of alignment with soul, for that is when negative things happen to us and others. This is the state of immaturity we call *evil*.

Pilgrimage Action 17
The Healing Pool—Visualization

+ Visit a pool or a body of living water, such as a river or stream, where it is safe to linger. Sit by the water's edge and use your breath to relax.

✦ When you feel calm, allow your mind to move into your solar center. Bring to mind any form of mental paralysis, stagnation, or resistance to change that you would like to heal. The first thought that springs to mind is usually the one to deal with. Stay calm—you are the observer.

✦ Show yourself what you want to let go of, what has been holding you back. Working with the cleansing energies of water, ask the waters to receive this blockage.

✦ Offer it to the waters and imagine that the energies of the water transform the blockage and return it to you as the flow of inspiration and a positive force for change. You have learned from the earlier experience.

✦ Sit with what the waters have offered you while you imagine a glowing golden light in your solar center. Thank the body of water before you decide to leave.

It is not always possible to visit a pool or a body of living water. The following activity also allows you to work with the healing and cleansing energies of water.

✦ Fill a bowl with water. Sit or stand within comfortable reach of the bowl of water. Use your breath to relax.

• Put your mind in your solar center and let your attention extend to the palms of your hands.

✦ Hold your palms over the bowl of water, a few inches away from the surface. Visualize that you can breathe out through your palms to energize the water.

✦ After a few breaths, let your hands and arms relax.

✦ When you feel calm, allow your mind to move into your solar center. Bring to mind any form of mental paralysis, stagnation, or resistance to change that you would like to heal. The first thought that springs to mind is usually the one to deal with. Stay calm—you are the observer.

✦ Show yourself what you want to let go of, what has been holding you back. Working with the cleansing energies of water, ask the water to receive this blockage.

✦ Offer the blockage to the water and imagine that the water's energies transform the blockage and return it to you as the flow of inspiration and a positive force for change. You have learned from the earlier experience.

✦ Sit with what water has offered you while you imagine a glowing golden light in your solar center. To complete the activity, thank the water in the bowl before you dispose of it.

Combatting Illusion and Delusion

The role of the mind is to build a personality so that the person can function within the family and other groups. Because we perceive via the conditioned mind, what we perceive is often an illusion of reality. The illusion is that we do not perceive the spiritual reality of the world, of other people, or even of ourselves. The *real* is what is perceived by an unconditioned mind. Soul's guidance is to help us recover the real and to follow the way of the heart. The method is very simple, but the practice of heart-centeredness is not easy.

When you become anxious and agonize about something, you build an energetic cloud of negativity and despondency around you. This has the effect of keeping away those positive things that are moving toward you for your own good. At the same time, negative things are drawn toward you by the laws of attraction.

During your practice or when you are in touch with your heart center, you may have moments when you feel despair and despondency, that your experiences and impressions are delusions. These are feelings generated by the mind as it tries hard to divert you back to mind-centeredness. But once you learn to allow the flow of mind messages to pass through, without settling on them or reaching out to them, you can relax and wait for soul guidance. In this relaxed heart-centered state, you will know why you are here and discover what you came here to do.

When listening to the voice of the heart, the mental filter of conditioning has to be acknowledged and accepted. It can be changed. By training yourself to become heart centered, soul guidance can be received with as little mental interference as possible. You will often sense communications from the heart as feelings. With practice, you will be able to distinguish between feelings generated by the mind and those that are the heart's voice. The heart's voice is always positive and constructive. It is the voice of unconditional love.

Happiness

The primary purpose of mind is to celebrate the sacred and to bring this to our awareness. The secondary purpose of mind is to bring physical happenings to our awareness. Through our conditioning, the secondary function tends to dominate while the primary function almost disappears. This why we do not know who we really are.

The personality seeks happiness in life, but when it is only operating with the secondary function of mind, true and deep happiness may be elusive. The drive to be happy is a motivation that is fundamental in humans. It arises from the mind's messages about our wants and desires and the fear of unhappiness and suffering. Mind has persuaded us that if we get what we want and desire we will be happy and if we do not get what we want we will become upset and unhappy. The worlds of marketing and advertising rely on this! Unconditional love in the solar center exposes these concepts as deep-rooted illusions.

A central tenet of Buddhism is that all action stemming from the wants and desires of the personality alone ends in suffering. The Inner Circle Teachings go further to state that action stemming from alignment with soul brings emotional balance and so happiness.

War and Peace

Mind's assurance that fear-based action is the solution to survival leads to struggle—between humans, between humans and the natural world, and between humans and the drive to exploit the planet. The outcome of these struggles is war. War is the presence of fear and the absence of love. Peace is not simply the absence of war; peace is the presence of love and the absence of fear—the presence of heart-centeredness and an end to the domination of conditioned minds.

Sacred Mind

When mind is trained to facilitate the expression of the sacred, it becomes sacred mind. Mind and heart working together in this way is not pie in the sky, the stuff of nonachievable dreams. Every day we see proof of mind in the service of soul. Recall the loving attention of anyone in the caring professions, the medical profession, the fire, police, rescue, and ambulance services. Such proof is shown through those who offer loving help to family and friends, to those in need or distress, through talking to another, passing the time of day, giving a smile, offering a reassuring touch. With the heart and mind in tandem, soul demonstrates unconditional love in the solar center in action.

10

LOVE IS GREEN

The Heart Center

*The seven life-breaths are born from Brahman (Oneness),
and the seven lights and kinds of fuel, and the seven
oblations and the seven worlds in which the life-breaths
move within their dwelling place of the secret heart, seven
and seven.*

MUNDAKA UPANISHAD (2.1.8)

WE HAVE COME TO the bridge between physical and spiritual
being. It is time to pause. The initiations we have passed through on
our journey have brought us through the base, sacral, and solar centers
to the heart center. The midpoint of the subtle energy system, the heart
is at the core of the Inner Circle Teachings. Unconditional love and all
issues around love in our lives are processed here. Soul is designed to
receive the energies of Oneness as unconditional love. It is soul's presence in the heart that makes it the balance point of the system.

With the practice of heart-centeredness, the heart center now
has the added function of overseeing the balance of each center as it
responds to the energies of unconditional love. Balance is about combining the two aspects of our lives—the physical and the spiritual—so

that we have strong links with both, not just one or the other. Once balance is established, the functions of each center are extended. The centers below the heart are now directly concerned with how the body, emotions, and mind are linked to soul's purpose and soul's voice. The three centers above the heart begin to process the activities of soul in terms of the expression of Oneness and soul's part in this expression.

The heart center processes the benevolence of the universe in terms of everything that we need to live. But as we have seen, lack of heart-centeredness creates illusions in the other centers. When we see love in its true form as the unconditional expression of Oneness, we experience that love manifests as beauty, kindness, compassion, forgiveness, truth, and wisdom. As we listen to the voice of soul, our eyes are opened to the vastness of love.

The heart links the two aspects of our being—soul and personality, spirituality and physicality—but society and education do not include the heart and the role of the heart in life, so that in our consciousness there is no link with the soul and the sacred. When love, caring, and compassion are devalued, the whole attitude to life in all its forms is affected. This has implications, especially for the raising of children and young adults, and how we care for people at the end of their lives. In so many societies, those who do care create little profit and so have little value.

THE FOUR-CHAMBERED HEART

The physical heart has four chambers: the right atrium, left atrium, right ventricle, and left ventricle. The two upper chambers, the atria, receive deoxygenated blood from the veins. The two lower chambers, the ventricles, pump oxygenated blood into the arteries. Each chamber has a valve that allows blood to flow into and out of the chamber. The heart valves keep blood flowing in one direction through the heart.

In assessing the awakened state of the heart energy center, it is helpful to visualize the center as having four chambers, something like its physical counterpart—but rather than physical places they are energetic states of being that reflect the qualities of a heart center. The four qualities are strength, clarity, fullness, and openness. Each quality interacts with the other three, and together the four qualities create the ideal functioning heart center.

A strong heart is a heart of courage and bravery, a heart that empowers us to stand up for ourselves and what we are, and to defend others who need our help in any way. If you feel doubtful in this area of the heart, lacking in courage, the Pilgrimage Action presented below will remedy the situation.

A clear heart is free from lack of trust, lack of self-confidence. It knows how to make balanced decisions and how to act. If you feel confused, or lack clarity in this area of the heart, the Pilgrimage Action presented below will remedy that situation.

A full heart is a heart that can give without counting the cost, knowing that its fullness cannot be emptied by giving. If you feel half-hearted, or have feelings of needing to hold back in this area of the heart, the Pilgrimage Action presented below will remedy the situation.

An open heart sees its oneness with all others. It does not react to the fears and prejudices of the conditioned mind and does not seek the mind's criticism or judgments. Again, if you feel doubtful in this area of the heart, closed or defensive, perhaps finding yourself focusing on what does not work, the Pilgrimage Action presented below will remedy the situation.

All four heart-center qualities contribute in equal measure to the energy that manifests as unconditional love and spontaneous action. There are times in life when you may need to act spontaneously, or in any of the ways that each quality represents. Regular assessment will maintain a fully functioning heart center. By acting like the valves of the physical heart, soul encourages us to look at how freely each quality is flowing in our life at the moment of assessment. Each time we intend to practice heart-centeredness, we can make a quick check to see whether we have the four qualities in place. We need to perform this check before continuing on our journey.

✳ Pilgrimage Action 18
Maintaining a Fully Functioning Heart Center

You can be in any place to make your assessment; you can stand, sit, or be lying down. Just make sure you are in a comfortable place where you will not be disturbed and where you can relax for the duration of the activity.

+ Use your breathing to relax your body, then breathe normally. Put your hand over your heart center to help you focus.
+ Remind yourself of the four energetic qualities that the balanced and awakened heart center needs: strength, clarity, fullness, and openness.
+ Visualize your heart center as having four chambers, each containing one of the four essential qualities. They will appear to your inner vision as light, and you are going to look at each chamber in turn.
+ If the light, or your sense of atmosphere, in the chamber seems gray, foggy, or dim, you can take the remedial activity to restore any or all of the qualities.
+ Look into the top right, strong chamber to "see" if the light appears clear and bright. If not, visualize that you can breathe life force into this section of your heart center. Breathe gently into the strong chamber until the cloudiness disappears and light is restored.
+ When you feel ready, move your focus to the next chamber. Look into the top left, clear chamber. What do you see? Does the light appear clear and bright? If not, use your breath to breathe life force into this section of your heart center to restore clarity.
+ When you feel ready, move your focus to the next chamber, below the two top chambers. Look into the lower right, full chamber. Does the light appear clear and bright? If not, use your breath to breathe life force into this section of your heart center to restore the heart's quality of fullness.
+ When you feel ready, move your focus to the next lower chamber. Look into the lower left, open chamber to see if the light in it appears clear and bright. If not, use your breath to breathe life force into

this section of your heart center to restore the heart's quality of openness.

✦ With your body relaxed and breathing normally, see your fully functioning heart center surrounded by and emanating a bright green light.

After performing this activity, your heart center is now fully attuned to giving and receiving love. Some people have a problem with receiving love. While they are able to give love, earlier experiences may have led them to deny their own need for love. The activity will help them correct the illusion and open up to receiving love. Everybody needs love.

THE PROTECTING HEART

To follow the promptings of the heart you must discover your courage, faith, strength, and conviction. All these are qualities that every heart possesses. Heart-centeredness is a protection against negativity. When negativity is directed at you, or just out there, it cannot penetrate the heart center. Instead negativity is repelled. On the other hand, when love is directed at you or around you, it is received by the heart center because it is a similar vibration. Being heart centered is also a defense, but not in the sense of a fear-based reaction, such as the need to be defended.

If you need to deal with those whom you fear, first recall that all beings have within them the soul. All beings are part of sacred creation, no matter how they may appear. The ego personality may override the impulses of love, compassion, and kindness, but this cannot destroy the spiritual reality within. The guidance of this reality can be contacted at any time, in any place, at any moment.

THE HEALING HEART

The Inner Circle Teaching is that there is actually only one healing: healing the effects of disconnection from Oneness/God. All other healing stems from this. Of course we wish others to be well and whole, but healing is about relieving the deep basis behind all pain and suffering. When healing is requested, the healer has to be sensitive to the person's readiness to accept the truth of healing—but in the process of relieving suffering, all healing will help a person reconnect with their spiritual reality. This will happen whether or not the person is conscious or unconscious of healing's underlying positive effects. The healer's path of service is a soul-based activity so that the healer's conscious connection to the Source also benefits the healer. In this sense, each person needing help provides opportunities for the expression of soul.

The restoration of wellness depends upon a return to spiritual harmony. The root of many diseases, and all dis-ease, is a loss of harmony between the ego-personality and the sacred. The restoration of harmony is not a cure, the procedures are not aimed at the ailment or to make the person feel better, or even to function better. The underlying aim of healing is the restoration of harmony. The disappearance of the condition, disability, or ailment is then a by-product of the restoration of harmony.

Unconditional love in the solar center reveals that we have such a problem with the fact of duality that much human energy is devoted to creating and sustaining happiness, with the pursuit of happiness as the goal of life. We have come to see unhappiness as a bad thing rather than the "companion" to happiness. Heart-centeredness suggests that if we were to reassess our problem with duality, we might well adjust our concepts of healing, healer, and patient.

For soul, there is nothing wrong with you. But from where you are now, you may feel that there is something wrong, especially if you are in pain. Pain is often a means of alerting us that it is time, right now, to listen to the voice of soul within the body. By listening in sacred silence to the body, we hear it speak to us, just as we can listen in sacred silence to soul, to hear the voice of the heart.

We are all on the sacred Earth walk that is our pilgrimage. The challenge to the healer is to walk with conscious awareness of the sacred. While you walk your walk you need to be aware that you are in the process of being formed, moment by moment. This formation is being created by the soul and the creation that is you is giving out energy. This is happening in every aspect of life, moment by moment. When we are conscious of these energetic processes, the emanation we give out is one that heals. This is the mystery behind all great healers and any great healing.

THE LISTENING HEART

The *eye of the soul* is code for the sacred aspect of all our senses; this means that it is just as important for listening to be done with the heart as with the ears. The heart-centered way of listening has many levels. First you listen to what is literally being conveyed, while at the same time you are listening to what is being said symbolically or metaphorically, even poetically. You must also listen to what is being communicated at a spiritual level, or what is most hidden.

Similarly, the healer's hands can be trained to "listen" to the vibration they are encountering; even more, the healer's whole being is listening to the vibration that it is encountering. This level of contact, this communication with the heart, puts the healer directly in touch with how best to help the patient.

In the early stages of learning how to do this, it is essential to sense what aspect of self is dominant and not let the ego interfere. The ego-personality may give us various thoughts, such as "I am powerful, this feels good, I am happy, it is working." Feeling happy, for both healer and patient, is a natural reaction to the flow of unconditional love. But when helping another includes the need for the feel-good factor, real communication with the heart may become blocked. The patient does not feel the warmth of caring and compassion.

When we listen with the heart, no matter how brief our time with another person, we deepen the relationship. Our relationships become authentic.

THE JOYFUL HEART—
BEGINNING YOUR DAY

Nighttime is for dreaming, daytime is for living. When it is time to get up from sleep, give thanks for the day with spontaneous words, a blessing prayer, or chant. Use your breath to focus on your heart center. You can reinforce your focus by putting a hand over the center. As you breathe in, become aware of the sacred space of your heart center. Once you feel your thoughts or words have immersed themselves in your heart, rest in the silence of that space, allowing your breath to connect you to it. It is here that we realize how our prayer of blessing and thanks invites us to be conscious of the continuous blessing of Oneness.

The simple procedure above takes only a few moments and can also be beneficial when about to begin any project or relationship. The next activity celebrates your new day.

 **Pilgrimage Action 19**
Greeting the Day

When you greet the new day, you open yourself to the energies of the Source. As you will recall if you have ever watched someone asleep, nighttime and daytime breathing rhythms are different. By gently aligning your breathing rhythm to the rhythms of the new day, this exercise awakens all your systems to the new cycle brought by daylight.

Practice the exercise outside when you can, but it is perfectly all right to practice it indoors too. Here, seven breaths of greeting are sent out to the seven directions of East, South, West, North, Above, Below, and Within. At the beginning of a new day, you take in the energy of each of the seven directions.

✦ Either standing or sitting, face the direction of the dawn, the place of the rising sun (East). Use your breath to relax your body. Become aware of your feet and their contact with the ground. Feel your connection to the Earth.

+ Give thanks for the previous night. Be aware that the source of energy and the promise of each day is within you.

+ Feel the air around you. Become aware of your breath and the fresh air entering your nostrils and your lungs. Note how your whole body enjoys the breath of the new day. With this action, let your in-breath and out-breath be slow and gentle.

+ As you breathe slowly and naturally, raise your arms above your head, as if lifting them up to the sun.

+ In this position of thanks and greeting, inhale and visualize the life force in the air moving into your physical body and your energy field.

+ With your next breath, breathe in the energies of the direction East, the place of the rising sun. Exhale.

+ Turn sunwise (clockwise) to face the South, the place where the sun is at its height. Breathe in the energies of the South. Exhale.

+ Turn sunwise again to face the West, the place of the setting sun. Breathe in the energies of the West. Exhale.

+ Turn sunwise again to face the North, the place where the sun appears to have disappeared. Breathe in the energies of the North. Exhale.

+ Turn sunwise once more to face the East. Raising your head to acknowledge the sky, breathe in the energies of the Above direction. Exhale.

+ Bowing your head to acknowledge the Earth, breathe in the energies of the Below direction. Exhale.

+ Lower your arms and cross them over your heart center. Breathe in and acknowledge the energies of the Within direction. Exhale.

+ Enjoy this state of harmony for a few moments before resuming your everyday activities.

If you are able to practice the exercise outside, notice the world around you as you calmly take your breaths. Feel the renewal of your sacred connection with life. Acknowledge the other life-forms that may be present.

THE NOURISHING HEART

The heart center offers us opportunities to develop relationships with anything that happens in life. For example, we have a daily interaction with something we really do need for nourishment—food.

The Heart's Thanksgiving for Food

We have a vital *relationship* with our food because it is the nourishment we need to sustain the physical body. The body is designed to digest our food without our having to think about it. We don't have to be aware that our body interacts with the food—created through the action of the four elements of earth, water, air, and fire/light. Society reflects our lack of awareness and poor relationship with food.

Food is cosmic. Whatever you eat, whatever your diet, your food is your communion with the Earth, the plants and animals that have given you food, and the source of food, Oneness. It is in the heart center, where we enter into conscious communion, that we realize the true nature of our food, the miracle that is food, and how the multitude of planetary beings are fed in some way. Part of the miracle of food is that there is always something left, even if this is simply crumbs or tiny morsels—there is always enough.

The place of communion is the place from which thanks originates, so that the act of eating, and any ceremonial act of eating and sharing food, are acts of taking/accepting and thanksgiving—the two polarities of eating. Consciousness of the spiritual nature of food can make eating a time of remembrance of the Source and being with the Source.

The Inner Circle Teachings are that food is signaling to us about our spiritual relationship. We can give what we are; we will not "run out" of what we are. Sharing what we have is the way to show that there is enough, and any giving on our part can be a ceremony of communion and thanksgiving.

Food represents matter, the energy of spirit out of which the cosmos is composed. Through remembrance and thanksgiving, we can recall the primal presence of Oneness within food and drink. Food and drink *are* Oneness. Consecrated or blessed food and drink possess an energetic charge that contributes to the spiritual unfoldment of those who partake.

In the next activity, the heart center reminds us about the origins of all nourishment in order to counter mind's fear-based message that there might not be enough to go around.

✳ Pilgrimage Action 20
Healing the Fear of Want

+ Prepare a small snack and a drink of water.
+ Go to any outdoor place where you will not be disturbed.
+ Sit down and get comfortable. Look around you at the natural world. Be aware if any part of it is calling to you. Recognize that the natural world needs feeding too.
+ Review your own fears around "there is not enough." This may be about food, money, or possessions, for example. What is your greatest fear about the issue of want?
+ Put your mind in your heart center. Allow your heart to show you where your fears around want originate. Put your palms against your heart center and gently breathe in green light from the universal energy around you. If there is green in the natural world, imagine that it is sharing this color with you in the form of light.
+ Breathe in this gift of the natural world. The universe will always support you if you allow it, but your subconscious anxieties may block this constant, unconditional support.
+ Take out your prepared snack and drink. Raise your hands in blessing or hold them, palms down, over your snack and drink. Give thanks to the Source for your sustenance. Give thanks to the Earth, to the plants, animals, and humans who have provided your sustenance. Offer up a blessing on these providers.
+ Take a small piece of food and offer it to a being in the natural world—a bird or some insects, for example. Do the same with some of your drink. Offer it to the ground and the plant world.

✦ While you look around from where you are sitting, enjoy your snack meal.

As a follow-up to this activity another time, have friends round for a meal. If it feels appropriate, thank your guests for the opportunity to share what you have with them. Later, make donations to charity shops and the homeless. In your heart, give thanks for the opportunity to share what you have. Keep your heart-center energy flowing by celebrating both giving and receiving.

If you give yourself a small amount of spiritual nourishment, you will relieve a huge amount of hunger in yourself. When you share your spiritual gifts with others you will find that you can "feed" a multitude and there will be plenty of your gifts left over; you will never exhaust what you have by sharing. You have the opportunity to help others when the odds against seem too great, to care for a larger number than you thought you could in some way.

The Heart's Blessing of Food

Living things need nourishment, and centering ourselves in the heart helps prepare us for the first meal of the day. The digestive system, like all the other bodily systems, works at a subtle as well as a physical level with the food and drink we consume. The physical function of digestion begins in the mouth, as does the subtle level of digestion. The finest energy vibrations of the food are absorbed by the tongue. These vibrations then interact with the life force. The body needs the subtle aspects of food and drink and will find ways of alerting us if it does not get enough in quality and quantity.

Because food has been part of a living plant or animal, it contains a range of energy vibrations, including the vibrations that have been absorbed during processing. Blessing your meals expresses gratitude toward your food and clears your food of unwanted energies, if this is needed—and it often is. A food blessing can also bring the food's energies into alignment with your own.

Offering a blessing ensures that all food can be honored through your remembrance of the subtle link between your heart center and the centers of your hands. This link is expressed when you visualize breathing into the heart center and exhaling through your palms. The second aspect of blessing is that gratitude for your food can be expressed by vocalizing the heart's message. Start your day by blessing your first meal.

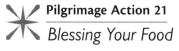

Pilgrimage Action 21
Blessing Your Food

+ Before you begin eating, bring your attention to your heart center and its link with the hands. Hold your palms over the food to see if your body really needs it.

+ If you sense that it does not, listen to your intuitive awareness and do not consume the food. This will probably not be the case with your first meal of the day.

+ With your hands held either over your meal or in a gesture of thanksgiving and blessing, take a full breath. As you breathe out, use your voice to bless and thank the food and drink.

+ You may also want to thank those who prepared it for you, or who brought it to your table.

Your spontaneous words, or even a sacred verse or syllable, may be more sincere than something said by rote on a regular basis without awareness. The effect of a blessing and a thanksgiving is always positive and beneficial. Enjoy your breakfast!

Blessing your food particularly affects its subtle aspects. The subtle energies of your breath and intention of thanksgiving link with the subtle energies of your food. A blessing is able to breathe life back into depleted food, especially that which has undergone commercial processing. Food should always be eaten with enjoyment and never with anxiety about what it is made of or where it has come from. Blessing your food can alleviate this anxiety, so go ahead and enjoy your food as a gift from the planet and the Source. When circumstances prevent you from giving thanks and blessing your food out loud, do it mentally. This can be especially beneficial when eating out, when you don't know where the food has come from or how it has been prepared.

Food is not just something physical; we are able to feed on the food of spirit. This assures us that there is always enough of everything, especially love. We have discovered a new key to living when we can express our thanks for, and commune with, our food and drink.

THE HEART OF REMEMBRANCE

Blessing acts as an important form of remembrance of our spiritual reality. In energetic terms, blessing is sending positive energy to a person, place, thing, another being, or even a situation. Thus it also has a healing element. Blessing is a form of gratitude in that it is an acknowledgment of the energy from the Source that is continually pouring into creation. Gratitude encourages the circulation of energy and unblocks and enlightens heavy, or dark, energy.

In the next energy center, the inhibitions of the conditioned mind to heart-centered communication and expression are overcome by the energies of unconditional love.

11

LOVE IS SKY BLUE

The Throat Center

All that lives, lives at the consent of everything else. All is gift. Life is gift and sacrifice. Life is prayer.

WISDOM OF THE AMAZONIAN MACUNA INDIANS

THE THROAT CENTER processes our illusions about how we communicate and express who we are. As we have seen, illusions about who we are and who we think we are reflect our conditioning over a lifetime. The personality's wants, desires, and need for approval, friendship, and love also contribute to the formation of these illusions. We may have communicated with others in the way our conditioned mind has suggested. This becomes how we present ourselves. Heart-centeredness exposes our assumptions to prepare the way for soul expression and soul communication.

If we have set out on the pilgrimage to heart-centeredness, the way of the heart, it is because we have put our trust in the guidance of the soul. Soul communicates its guidance through this basis of trust. Here we find the Inner Circle Teachings that trust depends on truth and authenticity. The energies of unconditional love initiate us into spiritual expression and being true, especially to ourselves. Thus, the challenge in the throat center is to be authentic. This means aligning our thoughts, speech, and actions with who we really are. Unconditional love in the throat center asks, Do you express who you really are, or only a part of yourself, none of yourself, a version of yourself, or a distorted aspect of yourself? What is your truth? Do you value truth or is living the lie okay?

TRUTH AND JUSTICE

Untruth accumulates energies like itself. Gradually, whole areas of our being and our life become weighed down with the heavy energies of falsehood and negativity. They have no power to do any good, even though this may have been our motive. Truth and untruth are at the root of justice and fairness, and injustice and unfairness. Practice of heart-centeredness will impact on the throat center to expose these issues so that you may often find yourself in a position to stand up for truth, justice, and fairness. This is when you need to make a quick check of your four-chambered heart center to make sure that you can hear its voice.

There may be times when you have suffered what you feel is injustice or unfairness and you have been unable to express your feelings of anger, sadness, or frustration. Situations like these can create a blockage in the throat center that can be felt as pain or discomfort in the physical throat—a lump in the throat. This can be relieved by the following activity.

Pilgrimage Action 22
A Throat Center Healing

+ Put yourself in a comfortable position and use your breath to relax your body.

+ Let the issues that have distressed you come to mind. Usually the first ones that immediately come to mind are those you need to deal with.

+ Check that your body is still relaxed and that you are breathing normally.

✦ Visualize that you can breathe a sky-blue light into your throat center.

✦ Do this slowly and gently, letting go of the pain or discomfort, the thoughts and feelings around the issue with each out-breath. You may cry—this is a natural release.

✦ Continue with the activity until you feel relief in your throat. Make sure that each breath is slow and gentle.

✦ If you become aware that your breathing is uneven or speeding up, it is time to stop this activity until you feel calm.

LETTING GO OF ILLUSIONS

The ego will fight to maintain its superiority, using all the tricks and wiles that the mind has learned over a lifetime. To avoid its artful promptings, we will have to let go of the ego's ulterior motives behind helping others, let go of anxiety about failure, let go of the need for the approval of others, let go of the need to prove ourselves, and let go of the voice of disapproval. The way of the heart is about relaxing and letting go. Just as we can feel the muscles and tendons of our body relaxing as we let go of stress and tension, so we can translate the feelings of relaxation and letting go to our thoughts and emotions. The throat center is aware that breathing is the key here, for the breath allows us to breathe out negativity, stress, and tension, and inhale the life-giving energies of the Source.

Turbulent emotions are caused by our reactions to life events, both internal and external—events that are first perceived by the mind. Mind's perception is immediately translated into emotional reactions and the throat center processes the expression of these. With practice, we can choose what our emotional reactions will be in any given situation. This is soul's message in the throat center. And this is how it illuminates the role of the throat center, for we will either express our creativity, our sexuality, and our joy through the filter of our conditioned personality or through a new awareness. We can discover a sacred dimension to our creativity, our sexuality, and our joy, and this is what we can now try to communicate and express.

You have the opportunity to overcome fear or powerful emotions, to do the miraculous, and to achieve the impossible. You have the opportunity to show yourself that these things are possible, to walk your talk, being who you really are and defying the image of who your conditioned mind says you are.

With practice, you can *feel* the Inner Circle Teachings in your heart center and with your whole physical body, where previously you might have read them, then logged them with your mind, or simply heard them with your ears. Unconditional love in the throat center intensifies its link with the sacral center, opening a new conduit for soul expression in all forms of creativity.

BREATH AND SACRED SOUND IN THE THROAT CENTER

The creative use of the breath and sound stimulates the throat center and its functions. Simple forms of vocalization unite all three areas of the throat center's physical concern—the ears, the throat, and even the nose. These simple, interwoven forms of vocalization have been part of human life for millennia. They are prayer and chant.

Our voice allows us to speak, sing, and say prayers. Unconditional love in the throat center has profound effects on the utterance of a prayer or a chant, as it does with speech. Heart-centeredness unites us with the magic and mystery of sacred sound and makes a space within us for the sacred. These sounds first affect our inner being and from there they flow outside to affect our lives as well.

Prayer

When we pray from the heart, we are opening our consciousness to the soul within. According to the seventeenth-century Welsh poet Henry Vaughan, prayer is the world in tune, and through prayer heaven is reflected back to us like an echo. The deepest purpose of prayer is to move us from the mundane, through the emotional and mental levels, to the spiritual. It is another form of alignment with the sacred. We can pray silently, or we can use the breath and voice to speak, chant, or sing our prayers. In these forms, we can choose sounds that resonate with us to balance and heal ourselves, to express the mood of the moment, or to lift up our surroundings and the world at large.

Chant

Heart-centered chanting of sacred words and sacred sounds ensures connection with the eternal now, where all dualities are united as Oneness. This connection makes the times of our ancestors become our times, and their moments of awakening, awe, and wonder, our moments. In many ancient cultures, such as the Hindu and ancient Egyptian, the chanting of sacred sounds and words was considered a fundamental science, and it continues to be a fundamental practice in Indian, Tibetan, Hebrew, and indigenous spirituality. In these cultures, pure, nonverbal sounds began the process of creation. This is the rationale behind the chanting of sacred words and syllables, or phrases made of a series of syllables—they are creative sounds. Heart-centered sound, prayer, and chant encourages integration or wholeness on all levels of our being, while removing what prevents integration and reconnection with the sacred.

Chanting has the power to restore vitality, heal, and connect us to the sacred through its ability to empty us of all the energies associated with stress and anxiety. This state of emptiness is a state of peace. We breathe in eternity, and we breathe out eternity. We are returned to joy.

The experience of chanting positively affects our breathing. The chant activity that follows encourages you to gently extend your out-breath so that your breathing becomes deeper. As you repeat the syllable of the chant, your breathing rhythm joins with the pattern of rhythmic repetition. This is why prolonged rhythmic breathing as a consciousness-altering practice is taught by most mystical traditions. Here, chanting is a form of meditation or preparation for meditation.

The way we breathe is fundamental to the way we feel in our body and the way we feel emotionally. The repetitive nature of chanting encourages deeper, slower, and more rhythmic breathing and causes the mind to relax. The vibrations caused by making the vocal sounds resonate throughout our bodies, down to the cellular level. Muscle tension relaxes, heartbeat slows, and blood pressure decreases. We experience a deepening state of relaxation as well as heightened awareness. Thus, chanting can create the relaxation response and reduce stress. This brings greater mental clarity with an accompanying expansion of all the senses. On a subtle level, the vibrations of the chanting breath encourage a greater flow of the life force throughout the system. The human rainbow shines brighter.

Many popular chants are in an ancient language that may be quite foreign to us. This can be useful, for the soul often seems to speak to us in a language we do not understand. Chants and mantras invite us to bypass the mind's need to comprehend, so we can feel the sound within us at the deepest level. Chanting or praying in a language that is ancient or not our own can open us up to the magical and eternal language of the soul. In addition, many ancient languages, such as Sanskrit, Pali, Hebrew, Tibetan, and Latin, for example, carry a special resonance because of their long association with chant and prayer.

From a healing perspective, chant is the vocalization of healing energy as well as being audible breath. The vocalization expresses the joy of life and gratitude for what healing power may bring to us, our community, and the rest of the Earth Family.

The Voice and Vocalizing

If chanting and sound prayer is not something you already do on a regular basis, it is important to prepare the voice and body. The following warm-up activity is the equivalent of tuning an instrument so that it is ready to play at its best.

✳ Pilgrimage Action 23
Preparing the Voice and Body for Chanting

+ Stand or sit so that the two girdles of the pelvis and shoulders are in line. Your spine should be straight and your belly relaxed. Hold your head up without straining. If you are sitting, place your feet flat on the floor in order to feel your connection with the ground. This is your connection with the Earth. If you are sitting cross-legged on the floor, this same connection is made via your base center. Rest your hands, palms up, on your thighs.

✦ Whether standing or sitting, use your breath to relax your body. With each out-breath, feel yourself gradually sinking into your pelvis.

✦ Relax your shoulders and the back of your neck. With each out-breath, let go of any anxieties or troubling thoughts, breathing out through your mouth. When you feel you have let go of any mental and emotional tension, close your mouth.

✦ Close your eyes, while remaining totally alert.

✦ Breathe naturally, through the nose. Keep your mouth lightly closed, with your jaws unclenched.

✦ Breathe gently into your abdomen and enjoy the feeling of being relaxed yet alert. Whenever you are in a sitting posture, this is the ideal state to achieve.

✦ Next, you prepare your voice, while maintaining a comfortable, relaxed standing or sitting position. Breathe into your belly and on the out-breath say, "mmm . . ." as if savoring the first bite of something delicious. Repeat your "mmm . . ."

✦ Choose a note to sing to. Breathe in slowly and deeply. With your out-breath sing a long "mmm" on the chosen note.

✦ Breathe in slowly and deeply. On the out-breath say, "ahh . . ." as if experiencing the first wave of a pleasurable sensation.

✦ Choose a note to sing to. Breathe in slowly and deeply. With your out-breath sing a long "ahh" on the chosen note.

✦ Breathe in slowly and deeply. On the out-breath say a loud "oh!" as if surprised.

✦ Choose a note to sing to. Breathe in slowly and deeply. With your out-breath sing a long "oh" on the chosen note.

✦ Breathe in slowly and deeply. On the out-breath shout "hey!" as if to get someone's attention.

- ✦ Choose a note to sing to. Breathe in slowly and deeply. With your out-breath sing a long "hey" on the chosen note.
- ✦ Breathe in slowly and deeply and, with your out-breath, growl like an angry animal.
- ✦ Breathe in slowly and deeply and, with your out-breath, howl like an animal.
- ✦ Breathe in slowly and deeply and make the sound "shh . . ." as if calling for silence. Start loudly and tail off your sound into silence.

Any laughter at the end of this warming-up activity will only add to the effectiveness of the session. You are now ready to enjoy the chant of the heart center.

✳ Pilgrimage Action 24
The Chant of the Heart

Like all the centers, the heart resonates to a particular sound vibration. This is the sound of the long vowel *ah*. The chant may be practiced standing or sitting.

- ✦ Maintain your previous relaxed position. Place one hand over your heart center.
- ✦ Close your eyes and breathe slowly and deeply. On your out-breath sing "ah" with a strong, full voice. As you sing the tone, release the breath slowly, via your mouth, first from your belly, then from the chest. Note which parts of you vibrate with the sound.
- ✦ Become aware of the space between your in-breath and your out-breath, and the space between your out-breath and your in-breath. This pause is the gateway to the subtle levels and energetic input from the Source.
- ✦ As you exhale, again make the sound "ah." Make your "ah" sound out as long as possible, without straining.
- ✦ Now as you exhale, sing or chant the sound "ah." Breathe in and exhale again, singing the same note without focusing on it. If the note

needs to change during your chant, this will happen without you having to think about it.

✦ You are making contact with the healing energies of heart-centeredness. This means that the first note you unconsciously choose will resonate with a part of you that needs healing. If your note changes quite spontaneously, the healing energies have moved to where they are needed.

✦ Continue chanting the sound "ah" for as long as you feel comfortable with it. Allow your session to come to a close quite naturally.

✦ Sit with the silence that follows the chant for at least two minutes before you resume other activities.

When any intentional sound is repeated for three or four minutes it becomes a chant. Chanting in this way encourages full-breath breathing. By controlling the air so that it is breathed out gradually, your breathing unites you with the chant.

Follow all sound work or chanting by sitting and resting in the silence—sitting and resting with the effect of the vocalization and chanting breath on your whole being. This achieves the ultimate purpose of the chant to align yourself with the healing energies of Oneness. As you sit with the silence and continue with your slow and gentle breathing, see if you can sense the energy generated by the chant inside your own body and in the space around you. Allow this feeling to open you to soul presence. Your journal can be used to record your chanting experiences. Where did they take you? What did they tell you? How did they make you feel?

We have discovered that working with the throat center, the heart center facilitates soul expression and communication. In the next chapter we discover how working with the brow center, the heart facilitates soul perception—seeing with the eyes of the soul.

12
LOVE IS INDIGO
The Brow Center

It is only with the heart that one can see rightly; what is essential is invisible to the eye.

ANTOINE DE SAINT-EXUPÉRY

THE BROW CENTER processes our ability to visualize, to sense intuitively, and to have subtle awareness. It also processes our illusions around these issues, such as the mind's message that it is not possible to see with the eyes of the soul, hear the voice of the soul, or to sense and perceive subtle energies. Unconditional love in the brow center creates the opportunity to experience through soul senses, to see the wonder of life and the world as they really are, not simply as a projection of the ego-mind.

SEEING AS LITTLE CHILDREN

I was traveling on the top of a double-decker bus to an outlying part of South London with my five-year-old daughter, Lucia. The bus stopped outside a parade of dilapidated shops and Lucia looked out the window. "Look," she exclaimed, "what a beautiful garden!" I glanced down and saw a patch of dry ground with a few straggling weeds and tufts of yellowing grass. Here and there the remains of takeout cartons jostled with discarded drink cans. Lucia's eyes were bright with happiness. She was seeing something I could not see—the vibrating energy and light around things, which made everything beautiful.

Many parents have similar experiences with their children. But the young child's view of the world may seem so divorced from the grown-up view that it is often dismissed. For many years I have pondered on the contrast between how my little daughter could see with the eyes of the soul and the way I was seeing. Somewhere a faraway memory was awakened. I used to see like that too; I had sacred vision, but at some time in my adolescence I had forgotten how to do it or had simply lost the ability.

When the Native American people of the Southwest talk about "walking in beauty," they mean being connected to the sacred and so having sacred vision. To remain connected is a person's first duty to themselves, to their community, and to the universe. When a person is able to see the beauty in every aspect of life, they know that they are in touch with their true selves and with Oneness. My daughter was reminding me that, for some time at least, all little children walk in beauty.

Walking in beauty does not depend on there being ideal conditions in the world around us. There have never been such conditions, yet history is replete with accounts of the sacred vision of the young. As a little boy, Thomas Traherne witnessed the horrors of the English Civil War (1642–1645). Yet in the midst of the bloodshed he received a unique vision that led him to write later, "The world is a mirror of infinite beauty yet no man sees it. It is a region of light and peace, did not men disquiet it."

The point is that we are all born with this way of seeing. Two questions face us: how can we rediscover it for ourselves, and what can we do to validate, encourage, nurture, and preserve it? An acknowledgment that sacred vision exists would be a start. Whatever our situation, it is time for us to realize that by not preserving the sacred vision of children, we are setting in motion the denial of the spiritual with its corollary, the alienation of the feminine.

Spiritual crises are present as illusions in each of the energy centers. The fundamental crisis due to the loss of sacred vision and awareness of the soul's purpose is the focus of the brow center. Today, we know much more about energy. We also know that our peace and prosperity and the plight of the world originates from within us. What we need to discover is that we are all part of Oneness.

If we have been groping in our own darkness, heart-centeredness in the brow center shows us how to see like a child again, how to reclaim personal responsibility, and how to deal with the obstacles blocking our path. This is what it means for us now to recover our spiritual sight. It is about seeing anew and about seeing what was hidden. We are initiated into spiritual perception.

But even though this has happened, there are still challenges from the centers below. The messages from the brow center will be examined by the mind in the solar center as well as being interpreted by the heart. The mind will attempt to make sense of all the new information, perceptions, and impressions that it is receiving. A part of us may wonder how spiritual perception is possible and if it can be a good thing. Surely such things are miracles that might happen to others but certainly not to us. Even when we experience our own link with the soul, we may still doubt it or disown it. If we embrace it, we will be challenged by those around us. Soul may have promised us a rose garden, but all gardens have to be cherished and looked after.

SEEING WITH THE EYE OF THE HEART

When the eye is directed toward something, it is the process in the brain and then the mind that makes the picture we see. But how we see the world out there and how we interpret what we see depends on what is happening in the mind. Different levels of consciousness perceive different realities. The only way to truly know something is to resonate with it. To do this we will have to do more than rely on the conditioned mind; we will have to engage the heart's perception too. This is done via the brow center.

Seeing with the eye of the heart center is accelerated by giving less attention to classifying, naming, judgment, criticism, and the use of logical reasoning alone, and more attention to immersion in the heart of the child within. Everything on the Earth and in the universe is a divine spirit in physical form. Every physical form has an invisible dimension and that invisible dimension is the dimension of the sacred. While we are developing this level of heart-centered awareness, we can speed up the process by imagining the invisible dimension present in whatever we choose to look at—we can use the faculties of the brow center to see with the eye of the heart, the spiritual imagination that embraces all forms of imagining and visualization.

The Diné (Navajo) people of the American Southwest refer to the life we think we know as the "glittering world." When the energies of the brow center are enhanced through heart-centeredness, our clouded vision is dispersed and we are able to see through the glittering world to the luminous world. We become aware of the emanations of everything as light—whether animal, plant, or mineral, including the elements of landscape and even the functions of climate. As the physical vehicle through which we can perceive these emanations, the body is not something to escape from or to be rejected.

VISIONING THE MESSAGE OF THE SOUL

Throughout and since ancient times, visioning has been the means by which the community has been reminded of, and put in touch with, the sacred dimension of life. Visioning has a history in many religious traditions as well as among indigenous cultures.

In the Lakota tradition, for example, when people find themselves at a crossroads in life, wondering which way to go, it is time to become heart centered. The goal is a spiritual vision. This is achieved through a series of carefully guided rituals involving fasting, dreaming, and physical trials. Though supported at every stage, those seeking a vision are thrown onto their own resources and their own connection with the Source and the spirit world.

Visioning is the effect of unconditional love on our inner vision— the vision comes from the spiritual level of our being. Where visualization is about *imagining* what is there by mentally creating it, heart-centeredness in the brow center is about seeing or sensing what *is* actually there. Heart-centeredness also shows that this visioning ability is present within each of us.

Visioning bypasses the conditioned mind so that the soul message of the vision is made available to us. The next activity does not demand physical trials, but it is designed to give you the opportunity to access a vision about a certain condition you may be aware of and to work toward healing it. The activity can be incorporated into your heart-centeredness practice.

Pilgrimage Action 25
Using Visioning to Help Heal a Condition

In this activity, your intention is to call on heart-centeredness in the brow center to promote a relationship with a condition that will make it easier for you to take action toward healing it. The condition can be physical, mental, or emotional.

+ Either sit on a chair with your feet flat on the floor or lie on the ground on your back. Make yourself comfortable in either position. Use your breath to relax your body.

+ Close your eyes and focus on your breath and breathing. Use your out-breath to release any tension you may feel. You are becoming calmer and more relaxed with every out-breath.

+ Put your attention in your heart center to access soul guidance. This is your intention. Use your breathing to relax into the center.

✦ Now move your attention to your brow center and use your breathing to relax into the brow center.

✦ Without grasping at it, let the condition come to mind that you would like to work with. Let this condition be present to your awareness without directing any energy to it.

✦ If you experience the condition in your body, place your hands there. Notice if you feel compelled to put your hands anywhere else on your body. Let your hands find where they want to rest.

✦ Your breathing will show you that you can be present in a relaxed way with this condition, with any pain or discomfort, and with any thoughts or feelings that may arise. Allow your breathing to help you stay calm and relaxed.

✦ Invite an image to come to mind that relates to the condition in some way. You may want to ask soul, "What do I need to know?" or "Show me what I need to see."

✦ Staying calm and relaxed, allow the image to appear. It may take a few moments.

✦ Spend time with the image and try not to grasp at it. Be a detached observer, without needing to understand the image or to work it out at this stage.

✦ Notice the details about the image. Spend as long as feels comfortable with the image. It will signal when it is time to let go of it by gradually fading away.

✦ Without trying to hold on to the image, let it slip away. You can help this process with your out-breath.

✦ Give thanks to your brow center, where the heart has been facilitating soul perception. Bring your attention back to your breath and your breathing. With every in-breath, allow yourself to gently return to a normal wakened state. With every out-breath, let go of the visioning.

✦ Gradually become aware of your physical body and your surroundings.

✦ Open your eyes and spend a few minutes relating to your surroundings.

Through the process of allowing an image of a specific condition to come to mind, you are making a relationship with the condition. This can be a great catalyst to initiate healing. You may want to illustrate your image in your journal in order to record the experience and to continue working with the image and its unique message.

As your experience with this activity demonstrates, the unconditional love of heart-centeredness in the brow center facilitates soul perception. In the next chapter we discover how, working with the crown center, the heart facilitates our ability to transcend the body, emotions, and mind to experience Oneness.

13

LOVE IS VIOLET

The Crown Center

We live at the edge of the miraculous.

HENRY MILLER

THE CROWN CENTER welcomes the triumphant, joyful arrival of the pilgrim. Located above the head, the crown center sits at the top of the subtle energy system and is the gateway between physical and spiritual reality. The brow center permits and oversees access to the crown. It ensures that we are equipped to meet our Selves in the crown center.

The crown center processes our illusions about the reality of soul, spiritual reality, and the reason for our existence. Heart-centeredness in the crown center is experienced as our direct connection with the Source/Oneness as we are initiated into the transcendent. While the heart center is the place of soul and soul guidance, the crown center is the place of spiritual Light (the energetic presence of the Source) and access to the Light.

The Inner Circle Teachings describe someone who is totally disconnected from their spiritual reality as living an unreal life in which their soul cannot express their sacred reality. The promise of the crown center is that because of our oneness with the Source, it is always possible to reconnect and to become truly alive. We can let go of the past and be born anew. This is the meaning of resurrection.

RESURRECTION

The Greek word for resurrection, *anastasis,* also means awakening, so the ancient word for resurrection has within it the notion of a spiritual awakening. From soul's point of view resurrection symbolically represents our waking up to the reality of our own soul from a state of unknowing. The ancient mysteries considered this state as similar to being dead so that awakening was a true resurrection—rising from the dead. "You are asleep, dreaming dreams. Wake up and return!" urges the fourth-century tractate "The Concept of Our Great Power" (*The Nag Hammadi Library* 6.4.40). Our "great power" is the knowledge that we are spiritual beings, souls, living a human life. The earlier Christian miracle story of Lazarus being raised from the dead can be seen as an allegory for spiritual rebirth through initiation.

The crown center invites you to look back. Your life of not knowing your own true reality may now seem like a time of sleep or even a kind of living death. With consciousness of your spiritual reality, you are alive and awake. You have gone through the struggle of confronting your illusions and of dying to your old concept of self.

FEMININE WISDOM—THE KEY TO KNOWING

To fully awaken we need feminine wisdom—the state of knowing that comes from accessing the heart for soul guidance. This is not an intellectual knowing but the *experience* of Oneness, or the soul, within one's heart, enabling a person to say, "I do not believe, I know."

The crown center monitors the four essential qualities of the heart (see chapter 10) and the readiness of the subtle energy system to receive unconditional love. When we open our heart to a person or any object, we enter into relationship with that person or object and we experience a change in our being as a result. Openheartedness accords with the rhythms of Nature—they are fluid not stagnant, ongoing not finite, a source of infinite activity, able to transform. Thus opening the heart to another person occurs as a function of feminine wisdom. It is a mutual, reciprocal movement that happens on all levels, whether or not these movements are seen or unseen, spoken or unspoken, sensed or unfelt. Like falling in love, where we seek to become one with the other, the movement of feminine wisdom is in fact the soul revealing itself to us as a permanent state of oneness. This experience of deep knowing, grounded as it is in wisdom, is an erotic event where we sense that we *are* the experience of knowing and intimately joined with it. Feminine wisdom may be interpreted by the mind as knowledge, but it is knowledge that can only be gained through the way of the heart. Those who experience the deep knowing of feminine wisdom do not *have* power, they embody it.

POLARITY AND SUFFERING

The Inner Circle Teachings show that feminine wisdom embraces and accepts the polarity within physical life. If there is pleasure, there will be pain. If there is suffering, there will also be happiness. Happiness cannot last forever, but neither can pain and suffering. War cannot last forever, and if the absence of war is peace, then that state cannot last forever either. If there is life, there is death. If there is pleasure, there is pain.

These last, difficult to accept, dualities have exercised human minds for all of recorded time. Whenever there is war, disaster, death, pain, and suffering, the cry is, "Why does God allow it?" Or simply, "Why?" But we never hear, "Why does God allow pleasure? Why is there beauty? Why is there happiness?" Inner Circle Teachings have a simple answer and that is difficult for most people to accept too— God/Source/Oneness *is* us, *is* you and me. If you are suffering, God is suffering. God is ant, bird, tree, flower, animal, fish—denizens of land, water, and air—known and unknown. God is each and every human being. As any physicist will testify, the physical universe exists according to laws of being. If these were radically changed to suit the needs, whims, or cries of humans, the universe would disappear. This is how it is.

The sooner we can come to terms with and accept that there is no separation between God/Oneness and All That Is, on every level of being, in all universes, the sooner we will come to terms with and accept the meaning of suffering. Suffering is either caused by human, geological, or climatic activity. It is not a punishment from God, the gods, or from any "heavenly" agency. Whether we like it or not, rail against it or not, suffering is part of the duality and flow of life. It is a facet of physicality.

Any condition can be seen as an opportunity for reconnection with soul reality. This is why it is common for many who suffer to look for the spiritual in life with perhaps an unconscious realization that an opportunity for reconnection has presented itself. When this happens, suffering can be life changing in a very positive way.

ONENESS BRINGS A NEW MORALITY

If living our oneness became the norm, a new morality would appear that has nothing to do with any religious strictures. If we are all one then we cannot kill, injure, or harm another; we cannot steal from or cheat another; we would have to look after everyone in all societies, without exception. If we are one with All That Is, then in taking from another, we are taking from ourselves; in harming another, we are harming ourselves. With this understanding, there would be tolerance of others, care and compassion for others. Society would see caring for all the distressed, disabled, poor, sick, and bereaved as part of a healthy society. Nations could not go to war. Borders and passports would become unnecessary. Weapons, spies, and secrets would become redundant. World poverty and deprivation would be addressed by the rich. No company would despoil or exploit any part of the world. A new regard and respect for the natural world and the planet in general would come about, bringing great changes in attitudes and behavior at local, national, and global levels.

At the crown center, soul guidance is that practicing oneness may sound like an impossible dream to minds, but hearts know that the future of the human race and the planet is in jeopardy if current goals and ways of being continue. The laws of energy are clear: each individual that tries their best to follow their heart's guidance on how to live with oneness will send out a positive ripple into the world, and this ripple will have a positive effect.

Justice and Injustice

For certain religions, the fate of evildoers is sorted: they go to hell, or they will suffer punishment for an eternity, or they will come back to go through the suffering they inflicted on others in a previous life. For those who believe that everything ends when we die, there could be a problem. How do we come to terms with all those who have killed, tortured, or harmed others and never been brought to justice, never paid for their crimes—with all those who have suffered or suffered injustice and never had redress, apology, or compensation? Those who do believe in the spirit world may be faced with the question, What happens to the mass murderers, the torturers, the cruel, and the evil when they pass over? Where is the justice? Where is the fairness?

The Inner Circle Teachings are that when soul (the real "us") passes back into the spiritual realm with the energy traces of its last life, the personality and the body dissolve. What will happen to the souls of evil people is not a matter of justice or fairness; it is a matter of love. And what love would do is very often hard to imagine, but the answer is always that what will happen is determined by what love will do. Further, with the loving guidance of other spirits, souls are able to review the last life and decide on what needs to happen next.

Evil

Being human is having unconditional love manifest in each of the energy centers. The lack of love in any of the centers leads to inhuman thought and actions, contrary to the universal law of love and loving. This law is reflected in our concepts of good and evil. From soul's point of view, sin and evil are not moral notions. Heart-centeredness in the crown center tells us that they are the consequence of forgetfulness, whereby people may forget or be unaware of who they really are. The Inner Circle Teaching is that sin is best described as a misguided use of energy. It is everything that emanates from a total preoccupation with the conditioned personality and physicality alone and a total ignorance of, or disregard for, our sacred Self. Sin is a negative or heavy energy that can only cause grief and loss of life force, and its accumulation results in a denial of all that is sacred in life.

The misuse of the word *sin* by religious groups needs to be explained. For example, we are born sinful, says the Church. This is a terrible indictment and a denial of our sacred selves. We are condemned and made dysfunctional by such notions and such statements. But when, on reflection, we realize what a total preoccupation with the ego-personality brings, what a denial of our true self brings, then and only then is it possible to understand the word *sin*.

Another unhelpful statement of condemnation is that, being human, we cannot help being sinners. This again is a statement that is only understood with mature reflection and should not be uttered in the presence of the baby, the child, the young, and the immature. The crown center helps us make the connection between total identification with the ego-personality—with its self-centered wants and desires—and the current manifestations of the disharmony in life, such as the degradation, the disrespect, the cruelty, the disregard, and the unhealthy treatment of people and planet. Having made that connection, it is then that we realize how we are beings that have accumulated sin (negative energy).

Problems occur when a particular religion or cultural group teaches us not to take responsibility for ourselves but to depend on someone else, past or present, who acts as our savior. Such teachings give rise to guilt and disempowerment. The word *sin* comes to us via the Latin *sons,* meaning "guilt." Thus the word *sin* is frequently understood to imply a particular offense for which we should feel guilt. If guilt is the feeling we get when soul reminds us of our disconnection, it is a useful feeling. But feelings of guilt can arise from mental conditioning and are not a message from soul. Certain religions have contributed to the confusion with the teaching that to transgress religious principles is a sin, or worse, a "mortal" sin that can threaten our chances of getting to heaven. Heart-centeredness teaches that such notions only create anxiety and simply misguide us to lose sight of the fact that sin is a direct result of disconnection from the sacred.

When we have recovered realization and understanding, we can confront the energetic and mystical consequences of living without soul and the spiritual. Heart-centeredness enables us to cleanse ourselves of the heavy energy we have accumulated and reclaim our sacred birthright.

MOVING TOWARD ONENESS

Once you have established your companionship with soul as a welcome practice, you can move on to the ultimate challenge of the crown center: the experience of Oneness. People have asked me what to do if you don't experience Oneness or do not really know what Oneness is. "How can I understand Oneness when all my senses tell me that I'm separate?" These are natural reactions. Until there is a change in our consciousness, it is normal to feel separate from others and from the world around us. The clue is in the word *experience.* Oneness/the Source cannot be known or understood by mind. This must be accepted. Oneness is an experience.

During such an experience, you as an ego personality may seem to "disappear." You are only conscious of Oneness. After a workshop some fifteen years ago, Francesca wanted to share her experience. She was a social worker with a heavy caseload. One evening on her way home from work, she was so stressed and exhausted that she stopped the car and got out to look at the landscape. It was winter. The sun had gone down and the leafless trees stood out black against the distant hills. As she gazed at the scene, suddenly it vanished. She vanished. Her consciousness that she was simultaneously everything and nothing only lasted a few minutes, but it left her feeling totally relaxed and joyful. She felt renewed, refreshed, and knew that everything would be okay. She was aware that, as her individuality "disappeared," she had become one with everything that she was aware of. Those precious moments were followed by many others, each happening without warning in the most ordinary of situations.

The memory of them has stayed with Francesca, as all oneness experiences do. There is nothing to fear from them. They are not hallucinations, but stages in the process of merging your ego consciousness with your soul consciousness. As we have seen, small children are quite open to moments of oneness, especially in nature, treating them as a normal part of life. You may recall such moments from your childhood.

When I have asked people to describe their feelings at such times, they find that words are generally inadequate. However, a common feeling was that it was like being totally and unconditionally loved. The Inner Circle Teachings confirm that this supreme love is the gift of soul and the promise of the way of the heart.

My answer to the questions posed by our everyday awareness is that until you have the experience, try to think, speak, and act as if you *are* one with All That Is. See it as a fun way to begin the switch in consciousness. It may be very challenging, but you will soon see that it is the real basis of morality and the way to treat others and the planet.

Experiencing Yourself in Others

After having some fun with behaving in a new way, and backing it up with soul guidance from your heart center, you can graduate to the next Inner Circle Teaching. This is embodied in experiencing and then recognizing yourself in others. The aim is to help move your consciousness toward the experience of Oneness.

When you see yourself in another person, animal, bird, insect, tree, plant, even climatic features such as cloud or rain, it is a form of communication—usually beginning without words. This form of communication is possible because We Are All One. Recognizing oneself in another is one of the biggest challenges of the crown center. After recognition, experiencing oneself as another follows.

The key to your experience is to allow your perception to see and feel beyond or beneath the surface of the chosen "other." No matter how the other may seem to appear to you, it is a being of Light—a soul. When the other is human, try to recall that beneath the personality exterior is a soul being.

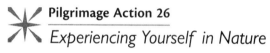

Pilgrimage Action 26
Experiencing Yourself in Nature

This is about recognizing yourself in the natural world from which you seem to be separate.

+ To begin, you can have the intention to carry out the exercise but the chances are that it will probably need to be spontaneous and depend on circumstances—where you are, who you are with, how you are feeling, and so on. Ideally, try to be on your own or with a companion who is sympathetic with your intention—they know when to keep quiet and not to intervene in any way.

+ Out in natural surroundings, just as in accessing the heart center, you need to be relaxed. Put your hand over your heart center. With your attention there, send a thought out into your surroundings that you want to identify with something in nature: a tree, a bush, or a plant of some kind. Remain relaxed and heart centered and wait until you feel/ sense a part of nature "calling" to you. As long as you are patient, it will.

+ Having heard the call from the plant world, direct your attention to it. First, sense a connection. Allow your consciousness to merge with the consciousness of the tree or plant. Do you recognize yourself as this tree or plant? If you do, can you experience yourself as this tree or plant?

✦ Another time, you can practice the same way by directing your attention to a tree or plant that first catches your eye.

✦ Practice the exercise until recognizing yourself in a natural form is not strange but something you can look forward to. Careful practice will reveal new things about yourself, about trees and plants, and about the meaning and reality of separation.

✦ In your journal, note how you got on with the exercise and what it felt like to you.

Pilgrimage Action 27
Experiencing Yourself in the Animal World

This is about recognizing yourself in the animal world from which you seem to be separate.

✦ Again, you can have the intention to carry out the exercise but the chances are that it will probably need to be spontaneous and depend on circumstances—where you are, who you are with, how you are feeling, and so on.

✦ Go out into natural surroundings where you might encounter a small animal or bird, or you could try this part of the exercise with a domestic animal. Make sure that your encounter is a safe one before you proceed further.

✦ Just as in accessing the heart center, you need to be relaxed. Put your hand over your heart center. With your attention there, keep the thought in your mind that you want to identify with your chosen animal, or with one you come across outdoors.

✦ Having identified the animal, direct your attention to it. First, sense a connection. Allow your consciousness to merge with the consciousness of the animal. Do you recognize yourself as this animal? If you do, can you experience yourself as this animal?

✦ Practice the exercise until recognizing yourself in an animal form is not strange but something you can look forward to. You are one with that animal. Careful practice will reveal further things about yourself, about animals, and about the meaning and reality of separation.

✦ In your journal, note how you got on with the exercise and what it felt like to you.

✦ Perhaps you chose a large animal, or a domestic-sized one, such as a dog, cat, horse, or a farm animal, perhaps even a pet. Next, you can challenge yourself to identify with something smaller, even as small as an insect.

✦ There is always some form of animal that you do not feel comfortable with. How about trying the exercise with that animal form? Remember, on some level, you are one with that animal.

✦ Use your journal to log your experiences and reactions.

Initiation into any mystery only occurs when you pay attention. It does not come by simply going through the motions of a ritual, reciting certain words, or reading certain texts. It happens when we pay attention to the ordinary and the everyday. A sense of awe and wonder encourages attention. In the early days of your practice, first pay attention to your own needs, later expanding your attention to those around you, to your community, to your environment, even to your planet. When you feel comfortable with your progress, see if you can relinquish old ways of thinking, especially "me" and "you," "us" and "them," as in you *and* the tree, you *and* the bugs, you *and* the rain, you *and* Nature. When you can, replace this old mindset with sacred presence so that you can say, "I am the tree, I am the bugs, I am the rain, we are all part of one another. I am not an observer of Nature, I am Nature."

Pilgrimage Action 28
Experiencing Yourself in a Human Person

When out in nature it can be a beautiful experience to feel yourself merging with a natural form, such as a tree. To do this with another human being is far more difficult. We really do seem separate from other people and there are people you definitely do not want to feel any oneness with. That's because we mostly see the surface personality. We rarely see the light of the soul within. Yet the eyes can always lead you there when the person is showing kindness and compassion, or any other form of unconditional love. We see more soul around us than we realize at first.

The activity follows ancient Native American wisdom to walk a mile in someone else's moccasins before you make a judgment about them or think you know them. This leap in imagination, to experience yourself in others, can also be an exercise in kindness and compassion.

✦ As with your exercises with plants and animals, you can have the intention to carry out the exercise but what will happen will probably depend on circumstances—where you are, who you are with, how you are feeling, and so on, though you do not have to be on your own for this one.

✦ Remind yourself that, in reality, you are one with the person you have chosen. Again, sense a connection. Now try to identify yourself as that person by trying to experience yourself as that person.

✦ This exercise is more than one of empathy—you are not wondering what it must be like to be that person. You are going deeper, trying to sense the soul of that person. It is this consciousness that you need to try to merge with.

✦ How difficult was that? In your journal, note how you got on with the exercise and what it felt like to you. After a few attempts you will have gained a new insight about other people and maybe gained insight about how you see or judge others. What does oneness mean now?

The Challenge of Other People

If you find that another person irritates you or triggers negative emotions in you, recognize this as a challenge to you and your practice. This person annoys you because you are seeing them through the filter of your own conditioned mind so that you do not see them with your heart's perception. They annoy you because you find it hard to recognize yourself in them, because you feel separate from them. In either case, you do not feel at one with them and you are not experiencing yourself, or the other, as Oneness.

When you are aware of such a situation, realize that the person is actually helping you. They are challenging your practice, telling you whether you are heart centered or not. They are telling you where you are in your own development as a heart-centered person. Such realizations can turn the situation around.

Selfish behavior, such as that encountered on the road, in the street, and in public places, brings similar challenges. But you can take effective action. First check your own heart-centeredness, then send out to the person you perceive as selfish. This can take the form of sending positive thoughts to them, or of sending light to them from your heart center, or surrounding them in a "bubble" of pink light. Rest assured that your positive action will create positive effects that will then ripple out into the world.

YOUR BIRTHRIGHT

We are born into a world that, because of Oneness, is as conscious of us as we are of it. It therefore makes sense to develop our closeness with the realm of spirit, with the whole natural world, with its landscape and ecosystems, with all the elements of climate, with the sun, moon, and stars. The network of consciousness that binds all the facets of life together offers a moment-by-moment invitation to be aware of, and communicate with, all the facets of life. Through them we can become aware of how much we are influenced by our conditioned minds. We can appreciate how every choice and decision can be one of feeling, speaking, and acting from the heart as ways of giving out our love.

Our birthright includes freedom of choice, but it is worth

remembering that before our birth, as a soul we chose to come to live on this Earth to express our sacred essence. This is the destiny of every human being, of All That Is. We are all connected and all is sacred. The experience of life is the soul's exploration and the soul's experience. From soul's point of view, it is the journey of life that is important, not the destination. When we link with this intention of the soul and make it our intention, the universal energy works to help and support us.

BIRTHDAYS AND SOUL'S MISSION

We each, as soul, move from a place of Light into the darkness of the womb in order to be born into the light of planetary life. When we pass from the body we leave a place of relative darkness to return to the Light. The burial of a body in the ground is the symbolic return to the womb as the being moves in the other direction on its way back to the Light. Our love of putting things in boxes, cupboards, and drawers echoes our moving into the womb. Then comes the fun of taking things out of the box, cupboard, or drawer. We may have the opportunity to see the objects, garments, and so on, with new eyes, as if seeing them rebirthed.

A birthday can now include a celebration of the moment in time when a soul incarnates into the physical cosmos as a soul being. Each soul comes with a mission to achieve, a task to complete. A mission is achieved and tasks are completed according to the choices a person makes in life. Your soul has its own goals that are set up before incarnation. They are the true direction of your life. Going into the heart center for soul's guidance will give insight about your true direction.

As we move through life, we can be aware that we are always in the process of being formed, always in the process of creating who we are, and that we are always giving out our creation to the world, either unconsciously or consciously. We are, in every moment, a great work in progress.

DEATH AND LIGHT

Our problems with life inevitably lead to our problems with death and what some consider as the end of us. In indigenous spirituality, wherever we are, we are surrounded by seven directions—before, behind, to the left, to the right, above, below, and within. Death, as well as the future, lies in the *before me* direction. It is one of the known, yet usually avoided, facts of life. Another, often overlooked, fact is that the *within me* direction does not disappear on the death of the physical body.

The body has never been a permanent organism or something that stays the same throughout life. We do not have the same body that we had at age ten and we have largely forgotten the way we used to think at that age. Nevertheless, the body is a beautiful illustration of the workings of Oneness. Since physical matter comes from the Source of consciousness, all matter is conscious. Through the network of consciousness, every part of our body is in touch with every other part. From the smallest molecule to the largest organs, every part works for the good of the whole: the soul's vehicle.

For the life of the body to continue, certain cells are programmed to die. A simple example of our daily unawareness of the necessity of death lies at the surface of our body. A good percentage of dust in any home consists of the dead skin we have sloughed off! Parts of our body are dying every moment as part of the organic process of renewal. Death has been with us from the moment of our birth, as a physical and energetic necessity. The crown center reveals its secret: that we embrace death, either unconsciously or consciously, in order to continue creating who we are. Can we accept that physical life and physical death, as aspects of being, are totally compatible?

The Inner Circle Teachings are that we were spiritual beings before we were conceived, we are spiritual beings on the planet, and we will be spiritual beings when we "pass over." The notion that *being* stops at the death of the body is an illusion. Mind may tell you otherwise. When you leave this physical life, you leave your physical body and its personality construct behind. They both dissolve. But subtle energetic traces of your life are now part of soul, part of Oneness.

The story of the soul entering into the physical body, living its physical life, and returning to the Light from whence it came is mirrored in so many aspects of life. Consider the daily story of sunrise, the progress of the sun, sunset, and darkness, with sunrise the following morning, and the story of the seasons with the apparent "death" of the sun, the light, and warmth, followed by a new cycle of birth. The seven colors of love tell you that you are Oneness/God in life and that you will go through suffering, death, and resurrection *because* you are God in life. Each individual life, each day, and each year tells the story of God in life, moment by moment.

The Inner Circle Teachings on death and physical matter are that all that is born, all that is created, all the elements of nature are interwoven and united with each other. All that is composed will be decomposed, and all matter will return to the origins of matter—spirit.

We have made the pilgrimage to the crown center because here we learn transcendence—how to move back into the Light after leaving the physical body. The various practices of transcendence, such as meditation, are a way of proving that we exist as consciousness outside of the physical realm.

Pilgrimage Action 29
Embracing the Light—
The Candle Flame Meditation

+ Set up a place where you can safely light a candle.
+ Sit nearby and make yourself comfortable, using your breathing to relax your body.
+ Light the candle and dedicate it to your spiritual ideal or any other subject that comes to mind. Say any prayers of dedication, thanks, and protection. Breathe normally.
+ Now look at the candle flame. Keep relaxed and maintain a soft focus. Notice the aura of light around the flame, notice the different colors.

✦ Close your eyes and see the whole of the flame light up your brow center. See it illuminating this center and gently opening it.

✦ In your mind's eye, slowly let the flame move down into your heart center. See it bathing the heart center with its light and gently opening the center. Any darkness or heaviness has left your heart.

✦ Now the light grows until it fills the whole of your chest. It spreads into your shoulders, down your arms, and into your hands and fingers. It spreads further to fill the abdomen and pelvis, moving down each leg and into your feet.

✦ Now the flame rises into your throat center where it illuminates this center and gently opens it. The light of the flame moves on to your mouth as the light of truth and trust.

✦ Slowly it rises into your head and fills it with light. It shines from your eyes and ears. All darkness and negativity has left your mind.

✦ The light in your heart center glows more strongly now and from your fully illumined body it shines out and around you.

✦ With your out-breath, let the light fill the room where you are sitting. Let it spread beyond the room to surround your loved ones, relatives, friends, colleagues, and even further to your rivals and people you do not like, further to strangers, and finally to all beings and the planet itself.

✦ Allow the light to fill and illuminate everything that you can imagine.

✦ Wait in this light. Be in this light. This is the light of the soul, the light of the Source of all things, all energy.

✦ Give thanks for the light.

✦ Slowly let yourself return to the place where you are sitting. Ground yourself by rubbing your hands together and rubbing your thighs, feeling your feet on the ground.

THE ONENESS EXPERIENCE

At the beginning of Dante's *Il Paradiso* (fourteenth canto) he stated that he had "the unspeakable experience of the supreme Light" (the light of

Oneness/God). But, says Dante, as we look back it becomes more and more difficult to describe such experiences, and more and more difficult to prevent the mind from intellectualizing them. He urges us to feel and sense the Light, both with our body and with the heart. The actual state of Light is then perceived as peace, a state of stillness beyond the understanding of the mind but found deep in the heart.

Heart-centeredness in the crown center creates a conduit for the input of soul wisdom and soul knowledge and the development of intuition. We learn to realize and accept that nothing is what it seems and that life holds greater depths than at first sight. The apparent veil between the physical realm and the spirit realm is the one we create in our minds. Our consciousness, our being alive, is nurtured by the constant flow of love as life-giving energy from the Source.

Heart-centeredness in the crown center leads to our reconnection with the Source of Life and why we are here as soul beings, with a body that has a particular genetic makeup and ancestry, all overseen and influenced by a soul-sensitive mind. Heart-centeredness will facilitate these reconnections for us through the impact of the unconditional love energy of the soul on the subtle energy system and the changes generated on all levels of our being. The heart center comes into its own as the premium organ of perception so that its upgrading dispels the clouded vision that can be detected in each of the energy centers. With heart-centeredness in the crown center, we are at last able to see through the illusion of the glittering world that each center has been dealing with.

The human rainbow is now complete and shines brighter than ever, with each color glowing with the Light of Oneness.

LIVING THE RAINBOW

- Unconditional love in the base center shows you and others and the world that the body, the Earth Family, the Earth, and the cosmos are a sacred creation.
- Unconditional love in the sacral center shows you and others and the world that creativity, sexuality, joy, and your inner child are a sacred creation.
- Unconditional love in the solar center shows you and others and the world that consciousness and mind are a sacred creation.
- Unconditional love in the heart center shows you and others and the world what the Source/God is, what love is, and that the Source and love are the same—they are One.
- Unconditional love in the throat center shows you and others and the world that heart is an organ of truth and soul expression.
- Unconditional love in the brow center shows you and others and the world that heart is an organ of soul perception.
- Unconditional love in the crown center shows you and others and the world that heart is an organ of transcendence. Heart-centeredness enables you to transcend the body, emotions, and mind, to *be* Oneness.

SUGGESTIONS FOR FURTHER READING

Angelo, Jack. *Distant Healing: A Complete Guide*. Boulder, Colo.: Sounds True, 2008.

———. *Hands-On Healing*. Rochester, Vt.: Healing Arts Press, 1997.

———. *The Healing Wisdom of Mary Magdalene*. Rochester, Vt.: Bear & Company, 2015.

———. *Your Healing Power*. Rev. ed. London: Piatkus Books, 1998.

Blake, William. *Complete Writings*. Edited by Geoffrey Keynes. New York: Oxford University Press, 1966.

Braidotti, Rosi. "Embodiment, Sexual Difference, and the Nomadic Subject." *Hypatia* 8, no. 1 (Winter 1993): 1–13.

Durham, James G., and Virginia E. Thomas. *Sacred Buffalo: The Lakota Way for a New Beginning*. Boulder, Colo.: Sycamore Island Books, 1996.

Eede, Joanna. *We Are One: A Celebration of Tribal Peoples*. London: Quadrille Publishing, 2009.

Gablik, Suzi. *Conversations Before the End of Time*. London: Thames & Hudson, 1998.

Kingsley, Peter. *In the Dark Places of Wisdom*. Inverness, Calif.: Golden Sufi Center Publishing, 1999.

Kumar, Satish. *Soil, Soul, Society: A New Trinity for Our Time*. Lewes, U.K.: Leaping Hare Press, 2013.

Machado, Antonio. *Campos de Castilla*. Translated by Stanley Appelbaum. New York: Dover Publications, 2007.

Marks, Elaine, and Isabelle de Courtivron, eds. *New French Feminisms: An Anthology*. New York: Schocken Books, 1981.

Moore, Thomas. *Care of the Soul*. New York: Harper, 1998; London: Piatkus, 2002 (new edition).

Okri, Ben. *A Way of Being Free*. London: Phoenix House, 1997.

Raine, Kathleen. *W. B. Yeats and the Learning of the Imagination*. Ipswich, U.K.: Golgonooza Press, 1999.

Robinson, James, ed. *The Nag Hammadi Library*. New York: HarperSanFrancisco, 1990.

Rogers, Carl. *A Way of Being*. Boston: Houghton Mifflin, 1996.

Rowland, Ingrid D. *Giordano Bruno: Philosopher/Heretic*. New York: Hill & Wang, 2008.

Tavener, John. *The Music of Silence: A Composer's Testament*. New York: Faber & Faber, 1999.

Tsu, Lao. *Tao Te Ching: Illustrated Version*. Translated by Gia-Fu Feng, Jane English, and Toinette Lippe. New York: Random House, 2011.

Winnicott, D. W. *The Child, the Family, and the Outside World*. New York: Penguin Random House, 2000.

INDEX